Praise for *The Wellness Whisperer*

"Raw, honest, and deeply inspiring, *The Wellness Whisperer* is more than a guide to health; it's a journey of the soul. Bianca beautifully weaves personal testimony with spiritual truth, reminding us that true wellness begins when we align our bodies, minds, and hearts with God. This book is a must-read for anyone seeking healing that goes deeper than the surface as it relates to caring for their bodies God's way!"

—**Katie Farrell**, R.N.
Author and Founder of *Dashing Dish*

"Relatable, kind, helpful, knowledgeable, compassionate, wise, and impactful—these descriptors capture Bianca's character as she skillfully weaves her personal story into a guidebook for achieving the ultimate healthy life. Bianca's prescription for wellness becomes even more powerful when paired with the personal narrative that underscores every word. She encourages you to be your best self, a motivation that envelops this stunning prescription for becoming fully you and fully well. While many how-to books seek followers for their programs, Bianca urges you to exercise your agency to reclaim the healthy life you deserve. I highly recommend this practical step-by-step guide to health and wellness. You'll find more than just body-positive psychology; you'll discover inspiration to live a fully integrated life. And isn't that what we all want?"

—**Cathie Ostapchuk**, M.A.
Catalyst, Coach, and Global Communicator;
Founder of Gather Women, Author, and Executive Coach

"In a world where there is an influx of health information, Bianca brings a clear focus and approach to it. What I appreciate about this book is that Bianca is not speaking about this from a hands-off approach but instead one where she lived it. Her vulnerability about her own journey brings a sense of groundedness and hope to the reader. She also brings in the most important part to any journey—our faith in God, a missing element in most health and fitness programs. Whether you are starting your health journey or are just in need of some encouragement, this book will give you the motivation you need."

—**Clare Smith**
Leadership Coach and Consultant

"I am deeply inspired by Bianca's journey and the way she has turned her life experiences into a powerful mission to help others. Seeing her embrace her calling and how she has used her life's lessons to uplift and guide others has been nothing short of remarkable. Her approach is deeply grounded in faith, compassion, and a profound understanding of the importance of aligning body, mind, and spirit. If you're seeking someone who is not only knowledgeable but also authentic and passionate about guiding you toward your health goals, Bianca is someone I wholeheartedly recommend. Her life and her work are a testament to the power of transformation, and I believe her wisdom will inspire you as much as it has inspired me."

—**Vanessa Hoyes**
Pastor and Reinvention Coach

"Bianca's book is nothing short of extraordinary. With her heartfelt dedication, she has crafted a resource that will undoubtedly empower and inspire countless girls and women. This book is more than just a guide; it's a testament to Bianca's courage and vulnerability in sharing her personal journey. Her willingness to walk such a brave path and turn her experiences into a gift for others is truly inspiring. The depth and authenticity of the book are what truly set it apart. I was captivated by how holistic and practical it is, offering not just motivational insights but also grounded, real-life principles that anyone can apply. The way Bianca dives into Scripture with such richness adds an incredible layer of depth that makes this book a profound resource for personal growth and reflection. Bianca has truly created something special—a guide that will nourish the heart, mind, and soul. This book is a treasure, and I have no doubt it will leave a lasting impact on everyone who reads it."

—**Kaitlyn Cey**
Coach, Speaker, and Executive Director of Inspire Our Nation

"As a life coach who's walked with hundreds of women through their health and healing journeys, I can say with confidence that *The Wellness Whisperer* gets to the heart of what's been missing. Bianca reveals the powerful truth that real transformation isn't just physical; it's spiritual. Her stories are relatable, her steps are practical, and her message is rooted in grace and God's truth. This book is a much-needed invitation to pursue wellness with God at the center."

—**Laurie Shopland**
Life Coach and Emotional Well-Being Strategist

"Refreshing, authentic, and deeply moving—this book is a raw and real account of Bianca's personal health journey. This is not a cookie-cutter health and wellness book. She has a wealth of knowledge and credentials, but the impactful part is her own transformation and that she has experienced and lives what she teaches. Anyone struggling to find true physical healing will experience the gentle invitation that it begins at a deeper level, discovering your true identity from your Creator."

—**Jasmine Dolotov**
Owner of Audience of One Fitness

Discover the Way to a *Healthy* Body and Soul

BIANCA SCHAEFER, R.H.N.

LUCIDBOOKS

The Wellness Whisperer
Discover the Way to a Healthy Body and Soul
Copyright © 2025 by Bianca Schaefer

Published by Lucid Books in Houston, TX
www.LucidBooks.com

All rights reserved. No part of this publication may be reproduced, stored in a retrieval system, or transmitted in any form by any means, electronic, mechanical, photocopy, recording, or otherwise, without the prior permission of the publisher, except as provided for by USA copyright law.

Unless otherwise indicated, scripture quotations are taken from the Holy Bible, New International Version®, NIV®. Copyright ©1973, 1978, 1984, 2011 by Biblica, Inc.™ Used by permission of Zondervan. All rights reserved worldwide. www.zondervan.com The "NIV" and "New International Version" are trademarks registered in the United States Patent and Trademark Office by Biblica, Inc.™

ISBN: 978-1-63296-874-6
eISBN: 978-1-63296-875-3

Special Sales: Most Lucid Books titles are available in special quantity discounts. Custom imprinting or excerpting can also be done to fit special needs. Contact Lucid Books at Info@LucidBooks.com

This book is dedicated to you, my friend.

Maybe we've never met, or if we have, you might be wondering who this friend is. The truth is, it's you—the friend I've known and the friend I have yet to meet. I say this because it's deeply personal for me.

As I wrote, I envisioned you.

I pictured the friend who feels frustrated—wrestling with their weight, their well-being, and all the mixed messages about how to care for their body. And I pictured the friend who's simply eager to learn how to integrate whole health into their life, seeking something that goes deeper than diets or fitness trends, something lasting and life-giving.

I imagined the friend who's curious about God and the one who already knows Him but feels stuck, weary, or unsure what true wellness really means.

So, my friend, picture us walking side by side on the beach with coffee, tea, or something refreshing in hand, having an honest, grace-filled conversation.

I pray that as you read these words, you'll feel encouraged, inspired, and empowered to flourish in ways you never imagined.

May God bless you on this journey.

Table of Contents

Chapter 1: The Mirror of Shame and Truth ... 1

Chapter 2: It's Not My Fault -- My Body Made Me Do It ... 15

Chapter 3: A Bloody Foot and a New Perspective ... 33

Chapter 4: Ditch the Cake but Eat Humble Pie ... 51

Chapter 5: Discover The B.Losophy Way ... 65

Chapter 6: Be Healthy: Part One -- Temple Ruins ... 73

Chapter 7: Be Healthy: Part Two -- The Wake-Up Call ... 89

Chapter 8: Be Healthy: Part Three -- Are We Just a Golgi Apparatus? ... 105

Chapter 9: Be Active: Falling Down and Getting Up ... 121

Chapter 10: Be Mindful: It Ain't No Careless Whisper ... 139

Chapter 11: Be Kind: Pay It Inward ... 157

Chapter 12: Be Beautiful: Those Stinkin' Cowboy Boots ... 179

Chapter 13: Believe: Call Me by My Name ... 199

Chapter 14: Be Inspired: Time to RSVP ... 217

30 Easy-to-Implement Nutrition Tips ... 233

Special Thanks ... 237

References ... 239

Chapter 1

The Mirror of Shame and Truth

Perception is a funny thing. What we perceive to be true isn't always true, but if we believe it is, it becomes our reality.

For the past few years, there has been one question I've felt uneasy about answering. It's a question almost everybody asks when they meet someone for the first time. It's a harmless question not meant to be offensive, and to some people, it's a question they don't mind answering. But for me, this question has become a source of anxiety—a question I have often tried to avoid answering, often fumbling my words when I try to respond. The question is this: "What do you do for a living?"

I imagine this question is no big deal for most people, but when you are a holistic nutritionist, personal trainer, and life coach like I am, well, let's just say that things have become a little predictable and awkward. The moment I tell people what I do for a living, it's as if I compel them to tell me about their latest diet plan—what they eat, what they avoid, or how they stay in shape. I don't often say much. I just smile, nod, and listen.

There's a reason I don't say much. It's because the conversations that follow often leave me feeling that I somehow make them feel uncomfortable. It's as if they think they have to explain themselves because they assume that since I'm a health coach, I am judging them based on their appearance or what they eat when in my presence. Although I have gone to great lengths to make people feel at ease, this perception of me makes me feel uncomfortable because I am not judgmental of them at all. I really love meeting new people and certainly want them to feel relaxed in my company.

That's why when I recently visited a new bakery and was asked the dreaded question, "What do you do for a living?" I decided to mix it up a little and replied, "I'm a writer."

Oh, you wouldn't believe the change in conversations I have been having ever since. I've gone from being someone who is viewed as judgmental to someone who is intriguing, and that sure makes for some unpredictable, engaging conversations. I've also become someone whose book they'll have to look for. I mean, it's true that I am a writer. I have had several articles and blogs published. But wow! If I had known the reactions I would get, I would have responded that way years ago. How refreshing it has been to change people's perception of me with just three simple words—I'm a writer.

But truth be told, being a health coach really isn't a bad thing. Neither is being a writer who writes about health. The problem lies in perception because perception can be a funny thing. How we perceive ourselves and others can often lead to how we judge others and ourselves.

> *How we perceive ourselves and others can often lead to how we judge others and ourselves.*

This Is Where My Story Begins

I became a holistic nutritionist and personal trainer so I could start my own business teaching people how to exercise and eat well. I opened a fitness boot camp and offered nutritional counseling to help women get fit and lose weight. At that time, I met with hundreds of clients and provided counseling, training sessions, and other wellness-related services.

I developed meal plans, fitness plans, and weight loss strategies. I studied various diets to help people learn how to manage their weight and lifestyle habits. I thrived on what I did for a living. I was so passionate about being able to do what I loved that I just couldn't get enough of all things health and wellness.

I became obsessed with learning and obtaining certifications to round out my education. I wasn't just a personal trainer and registered holistic nutritionist; I became a certified life and business coach, a fitness instructor, a yoga teacher, a fitness kickboxing instructor, and a Pilates teacher. I competed in fitness bodybuilding contests, ran marathons, and became a third-degree black belt in taekwondo. And while those may seem impressive in their own right, I wasn't finished. I still had so many goals to reach and was well on my way to being perceived as the expert health coach, owner of a successful business, and—unbeknownst to me—the woman who seemed to have it all together.

A few years into running my fitness boot camp, I developed a new strategy that would help people better understand the challenges they faced when struggling with their weight and health. This new strategy consisted of two parts. The first was the blueprint, which revealed how the body worked and why they were gaining weight. It offered logical, scientific insights into their health issues. I named this blueprint The Unhealthy Body Cycle. The second was based on my philosophy for healthy living, which revealed the solution to how to break the cycle and build healthy lifestyle habits. I named this philosophy B.Losophy—named, of course, after me, Bianca. B.Losophy, combined with The Unhealthy Body Cycle, provided my clients with the road map to success for how to achieve and maintain a healthy weight and lifestyle.

After years of trying, testing, and perfecting my newly created road map, my philosophy for healthy living proved to be the cornerstone of the new direction I was taking my business. I developed a fresh website with the intention of offering online programs. I also began writing this book, which is based on the principles of B.Losophy and The Unhealthy Body Cycle. But after writing a few chapters, I felt like something was missing. I couldn't quite put my finger on it. It felt like I had all the right answers, and it made perfect sense from a logical standpoint. If you do this, then you'll achieve these results. But I kept having a nagging feeling that there was more to it than the surface-level results and that maybe, deep down, I was withholding something. The question was what.

After months of contemplation, I realized that those nagging feelings were true, and I wasn't being completely honest. The truth was that when I presented my clients with my newly created road map, I danced around one very important aspect of health. This aspect was based on my faith as a believer in Jesus Christ. As a Christian, I felt that my faith was as much a part of my health as what I ate or how often I exercised; I just didn't know how to casually weave Jesus into a conversation. Instead, I said things like this: "Your beliefs or faith are very important when it comes to your health."

But now and then I heard a little voice in my head whisper this: "You're not sharing everything you know about health." At first I wasn't quite sure whose voice I was hearing or what this statement meant. Perhaps I was just talking to myself. But after hearing it time and time again, I sensed God was the one nudging me to be more specific, to share my faith more publicly, and to talk about how He had influenced my life and health. The problem was that I was afraid of what my clients would think if I started talking about Jesus right in the middle of a nutrition counseling or personal training session. After all, I wasn't running a Christian business. As long as people knew I was a Christian but I didn't push my religion on them, I could still be effective as a health coach, right? I reasoned that just because I was a Christian didn't mean I had to run a Christian health and wellness business. And honestly, if you're a health coach and a Christian, you don't need to combine the two. But in my circumstance, months and months went by, and that little voice inside my head wouldn't go away.

"You're not sharing everything you know about health."

Uh huh.

At the time, I didn't quite understand the full impact of what that statement meant. So instead, I chose to ignore it.

Broken to Pieces

Just as my new website was completed and I was developing my online program, some major life changes turned my world upside down. Within a two-year period, my husband and I watched four members of our family take their last breath. During that time, we had also just gotten married, started home renovations, and were engaged in a legal dispute. I had also become a stepmom to two adult daughters. This two-year period was an extremely stressful season in our lives and proved to be one of the most difficult and painful times of my entire life.

The effects of watching our family suffer definitely left its mark on me. During that time, I became very unhealthy. The stress of knowing you can't stop death is a difficult thing to face, even when you believe God is in control.

I tried so hard to keep a positive outlook, and I refused to believe that death would come. I prayed relentlessly for miracles and healing. As my husband watched his loved ones die, I prayed that the pain he was going through would subside. And yet amid all that prayer, I didn't handle things well. I'm not sure if I ever prayed prayers that were for me. It seemed like I was just trying to help everyone else. Looking back, it's as if I was saying to God, "Just help them. I'll take care of myself."

In addition to everything we were dealing with, unexplained aches and pains began to develop in my body that I attributed to stress. My eating habits became atrocious. I couldn't sleep. I was sad and depressed, and I struggled to lead my classes at boot camp with the same encouragement and motivation they were so accustomed to receiving from me. Slowly but surely I was losing my passion for health and wellness, and there wasn't anything I could do about it.

Throughout this two-year period, my body broke down. I visited countless specialists and had several tests, X-rays, and MRIs. I visited holistic and alternative health practitioners. I researched endlessly, trying to figure out what was wrong with me because the physical pain in my body would not relent. I could no longer run, practice taekwondo, or do the things I loved. Everyday chores became difficult. Losing my physical ability was heartbreaking both mentally and emotionally. My identity as a physically active person diminished. I developed frozen shoulder, a painful condition that restricted my ability to move my left arm more than an inch away from my body. Bursitis settled into my hips, and a mysterious pain took root in my lower left abdomen. I endured two years of blood tests, colonoscopies, ultrasounds, and a cancer scare, but I still had no answers for the origin of my abdominal pain.

In my exhaustion, I cried out to God more times than I can remember. "Why is this happening to me?"

I prayed for healing and took every step imaginable to heal myself of this pain, including massage therapy, yoga, acupuncture, and Chinese medicine. I took naturopathic supplements and tried counseling. I worked on reducing my stress levels and began eating better again. Yet still, the pain did not subside. In fact, it got worse.

As if that wasn't enough, I gained weight, and not just a few unnoticeable pounds. My clothes didn't fit anymore. Every few months I had to buy a bigger size. I became extremely self-conscious and wanted nothing more than to cover up my body and hibernate so no one would see me. I was embarrassed and felt shameful about how my body looked. I didn't want my picture taken, and I certainly did not want my husband to see me naked.

Eventually, I dissolved my boot camp business and lost all desire to continue as a health coach. I reasoned that if I couldn't help myself, how could I help others? Sadly, I didn't even recognize myself in the mirror anymore.

People asked me what I was doing with my time since I wasn't working anymore, and I felt judged. I told them I was writing my book, but I felt paralyzed every time I tried to write. I doubted my knowledge as a health coach, and I kept thinking, "How could a health expert with all these certifications let herself go?"

My perception of myself began to change with every pound added to the scale. But even though I knew stepping on the scale would make me feel worse, I couldn't stay away. Each time I stepped off, I felt defeated like a captive to addiction and filled with shame. Then the pity party decided to pay me a visit.

Everyone is looking at you and thinking you don't even know what you're talking about regarding health. Some expert! You can't even apply your own B.Losophy to yourself.

Look at you; you can't exercise anymore.

You're a failure. You have no business.

Everybody thinks you're lazy.

Your husband is supporting you because you don't make any money.

These thoughts, along with many others, consistently tormented me as I mourned the loss of who I thought I once was. Looking back, I had no idea that Satan had his grip on me. He took full advantage of every little insecurity I ever felt and blew them up so I was consumed with feelings of unworthiness and doubt. For all the things I felt grateful for in my life—my husband, my family—a million other things were going wrong, and Satan didn't let me forget them. Whether it was physical, mental, or emotional, it seemed I was always in pain.

And then one day I thought I heard something.

Pause.

"Who are you?"

Silence.

I wondered, *Where did that question come from?* Unsure of what to make of it, I brushed it off. But now and then I would hear that same question.

"Who are you?"

Silence.

Never really knowing what to make of it, I brushed it aside month after month like it was nothing. Every. Single. Time. Until one day several months later.

I was standing in front of the mirror half-dressed, blinded by tears as I stared at my reflection. The pity party came to visit me again, and I could tell I was in for a doozy.

It was then that I heard it again.

"Who are you?"

Pause. I stood still.

"Who are you when all has been stripped away?"

Tears welled up again. I shook my head from side to side until I broke out into a full-blown sob. This time, I knew exactly Who was asking these questions, and I couldn't hide from Him any longer. But I didn't want to answer.

So He asked me again, "Who are you when all has been stripped away?"

Standing there half-naked in front of the mirror, no covering up could hide how I was feeling, and I knew it was time to have a real heart-to-heart with God.

There in my bedroom in front of the mirror, I sat on the floor and closed my eyes. I began to feel the Holy Spirit, and it felt like He was massaging my heart. With every stroke of compassion and touch of gentleness, I found myself releasing all my insecurities and feelings of unworthiness. I talked about all the things I could no longer do and how I felt about myself as a result. Tear after tear, I complained about my inabilities, how unsuccessful I felt, and how unattractive I was. But no matter what I said or how much I explained, the Lord kept telling me He loved me. And the more He told me He loved me, the more I tried to convince Him why He shouldn't. But He never wavered. He let me go on and on until I was completely finished, and after I laid it all out, He asked me this: "Who are you in Christ?"

And suddenly, unexplainably, these words poured out of me: "I am fearfully and wonderfully made.[1] My body weight, shape, ability, and appearance do not matter. Success does not matter. You even know the number of hairs I have on my head."

I smiled through the tears when I heard a number and thought, *He even has a sense of humor.*

Then He asked another question.

"Can you still be faithful (and useful) despite your circumstance?"

I nodded and replied, "Yes."

Finally, healing could begin.

---

[1] If you are unfamiliar with the Bible, "*I am fearfully and wonderfully made*" refers to a part of Scripture from Psalm 139:13–16. They are comforting verses when you feel down about yourself because they remind us how precious we are to God.

The Missing Piece

Not long after that conversation between me and the Lord, He unexpectedly revealed to me the missing piece concerning my newly created strategy involving B.Losophy and The Unhealthy Body Cycle. Remember earlier when I said that I felt like something was missing every time I tried to write my book? Well, as it turns out, something was missing—something huge, in fact. It was as if suddenly everything made complete sense, and I couldn't believe what spilled out onto my pages through His guidance as I drew out the missing piece.

The Lord revealed to me that The Unhealthy Body Cycle actually consisted of two parts, not just one. Part One revealed the physiological struggle that takes place when you find yourself spinning out of control with unhealthy lifestyle habits. It's based on our physical health. Part Two encompasses our spiritual health, which is completely intertwined with our physical well-being. Our spiritual struggles are what lead to the physical outcomes we experience, which may not be so apparent when you are going through a health crisis of your own. Remember, even with my vast knowledge of health and all my certifications, nothing could have prepared me for this season of struggle in my life. Why? Because I was focused on the wrong thing. I was focused on healing my physical health without realizing that my spiritual health was at stake. No wonder I couldn't apply my own B.Losophy when I went through my health crisis. In its original format, B.Losophy failed to address my spiritual health. Finally, it all made sense.

> *I was focused on healing my physical health without realizing that my spiritual health was at stake.*

So what did God mean when He said to me, "You're not sharing everything you know about health?" On some level, I think I knew there was much more to health than what I was willing to share. The problem was that I was not obedient in sharing my faith, which was a necessary step on my journey to discovering the missing piece.

The Things God Wanted Me to Know

I was blown away once I recognized the gift God had given me. But even with this new understanding, healing didn't happen overnight. When the Lord revealed The Unhealthy Body Cycle, Part Two, it took time for me to fully surrender to His will. I wrestled with it for a while, trying to make sense of what He was asking, counting the cost, and wondering if I was really ready. But before He allowed me to share this revelation, He wanted me to live it first. If I truly wanted to heal, I had to be obedient to how He wanted me to do it. Healing was about so much more than recognizing a problem. It meant letting His way shape how I lived each day. And over the next year, that meant putting everything He'd taught me into action.

The first thing I learned was that in order for me to heal, I needed to understand who I was. Even after the Lord gave me this new insight, it still took quite a while for me to stop listening to Satan's lies about me and embrace God's truth.

In terms of my circumstance, nothing had changed. I didn't know what I was going to do with my life, if I would go back to health coaching or choose a different career path. I was still unhealthy and overweight, and I still felt unattractive. But it took repeated prayer and communication with God to look at myself in the mirror and love myself as the Heavenly Father loves me—a woman who is valued and loved unconditionally, no matter her circumstance or her appearance. That didn't mean I liked my reflection. It just meant I could still love myself and appreciate the work He was doing in me. The rest, whatever it would be, would come later.

Before that day in front of the mirror, I didn't know what it meant to truly know who I was in Christ. As a Christian gal, I could talk about my identity in Christ, but when God put me to the test, how did I respond? I thought I was the health expert with the endless list of certifications, the successful business owner, the woman who was perceived as having it all together. I placed my own personal value on what I thought others thought of me and what I thought I should be. But the truth is that God does not view us the same way.

We are cherished by Him for completely different reasons. He made every fiber of our being with intentional thought. He knows us inside out. He loves us more than we can comprehend. We are His children, and I think it saddens Him when we don't value His creation—us.

So when it comes to our weight, shape, appearance, and ability, why are we basing our self-worth on an external perception of ourselves? Why do we place our value on how we feel from one day to the next? If your weight is up, you feel bad. If your weight is down, you feel good. If your career or relationship is successful, you feel accomplished and loved. If you're unsuccessful or without someone, you feel like a failure.

This way of thinking is all messed up and not at all how God wants us to look at things. The Bible says, "Set your minds on things above, not on earthly things" (Col. 3:2). In other words, we shouldn't base our confidence on our feelings or circumstance. Instead, God wants our confidence to come from knowing Whose we are. When we do that, we can honor Him and feel good about ourselves, even when the reflection we see in the mirror is an unfinished and imperfect work in progress.

> *God wants our confidence to come from knowing Whose we are.*

The second thing I learned was that I had to fully submit every area of my life to Him, including my physical, mental, and spiritual healing. Ultimately, even though I was a health coach and had a wealth of knowledge and understanding of the human body, I was not in charge of healing myself. God was. And if I wanted to live pain-free again, I had to trust and depend on God, not myself.

I could no longer view my current state of physical health separate from the state of my mental and spiritual health. And even though I thought I was growing closer to God, had a committed prayer life, and studied the Bible, I somehow still missed this very important point. Submitting all areas of my life meant realigning my physical and mental health with my spiritual life. All strongholds needed to be broken, and I needed God's help to do it.

That's why when it comes to changing your diet, stress level, sleep, or lifestyle habits, it's not enough just to follow a plan that focuses on healing your physical body. One reason so many people struggle with a new diet is because they are trying to use their willpower to overcome cravings or lifelong unhealthy habits. But the struggle of going from unhealthy to healthy requires God's power through his Holy Spirit, not willpower through ourselves.

The Whisper That Became Loud and Clear

In truth, your struggle is not just a physical one; it's a mental and spiritual one as well. Changing unhealthy habits requires more than starting over on Monday. It requires more action than removing all the junk food in the house and working out daily. It even requires more than praying for weight loss. It requires coming to a place of true humility and acknowledging that you can't and shouldn't do it alone. You must rely on the One who loves you beyond your own comprehension, the only One who knows you better than you know yourself, and the only One whose true perception of you is accurate—your Creator, God. Once I learned to fight my health struggles using His holy power and not my human willpower, I was finally set on the right path to begin a new healing journey. And so, a whole new B.Losophy was born. Woohoo!

As I sit here writing this book, I'm happy to say I feel much better. I can move my left arm above my head, and I'm back to being physically active on a daily basis. I am not the woman I used to be, but thankfully, I don't have to be.

As I was humbled and strengthened, God restored my passion for health and wellness and gave me a greater understanding of discovering my true purpose. He placed a burning desire in my heart to share with you what I have learned through my personal struggle, and my hope is that sharing this will help you too.

If you're frustrated and feeling stuck regarding your health, weight, or lifestyle, I want you to know that you don't need to keep feeling that way. God cares about you and understands exactly how you feel. He is concerned about your state of mind. He does care about how unhappy you feel when you're not at your best. And He definitely does not want you to be unhealthy or weighed down by a misguided perception of yourself. That's why I'm on this mission to share with you what God has shared with me—the answer to how you, too, can finally reach your health goals, end your frustration with so-called proven diets that never deliver in the long term, and break free from the worldly perception of what healthy living really looks like.

You will have the knowledge, tools, and wisdom to live the healthy life He wants you to live, one that is God-honoring and God-glorifying. Because when you are healthy in body, mind, and spirit, He can use you in ways you can't even imagine! Let's get started, shall we?

Chapter 2

It's Not My Fault -- My Body Made Me Do It

I was in one of those cute little gift shops that sells trinkets and home decor. You know the ones I'm talking about. They're usually in the touristy part of town, and every so often, I like to go in just to have a look. Though I don't really need anything, browsing around is fun. What cute little mugs, candleholders, bowls, and serving dishes! Oh, and let's not forget those cute tea towels embroidered with sayings that only women can really understand such as "Cal-o-rie (noun) - A tiny little creature that lives in your closet and sews your clothes a little tighter every night." I snapped a picture of it and showed it to my husband. He smiled and began to walk away. "Hold on," I persisted. "Don't you think this is absolutely hilarious? I think almost every woman can relate to this. I mean, how many times have we woken up and suddenly our clothes feel tight? They don't fit. This must be the reason why." I laughed and winked at him. "Sure, that could be it," he replied, unimpressed. *Uh-huh*, I said to myself. *He has no idea what I'm talking about.*

In Chapter 1, I introduced the blueprint I created to help my clients understand the pitfalls they face when trying to maintain a healthy body. Since my primary focus was helping women lose weight, I wanted them to understand how the body functioned and why weight loss proved difficult. The Unhealthy Body Cycle was based on my expertise as a holistic nutritionist. It was both research-based and experiential, having worked with hundreds of clients during my career as a health coach. Time and time again I heard women complain of similar struggles, and I began to notice a pattern. They wanted to lose weight, but no diet seemed to work in the long term. They wanted to eat better or exercise, but too often they lacked the energy they needed. Their stress levels soared, and they were always tired. Their self-confidence was depleted as their weight increased and their clothes became tighter. Late-night cravings always got the better of them. And there was never enough time in the day to get everything done, let alone plan fast, healthy, nutritious meals that the whole family could enjoy.

As I began noticing some similarities, I knew there had to be a logical explanation. And that's how The Unhealthy Body Cycle was born. As I shared my blueprint with clients, I could see how it enlightened them. It was as if it had lifted a significant burden off their shoulders, and they could see themselves in this very cycle. Finally they had found the answer they were looking for, the real reason they felt the way they did—out-of-control and powerless in their battle against weight gain and low energy. But even more important than that, The Unhealthy Body Cycle provided them with the knowledge and understanding they so desperately needed to gain some peace of mind. There was a sound, physiological explanation for why they struggled, and surprisingly, it wasn't even their fault.

The Unhealthy Body Cycle Part 1

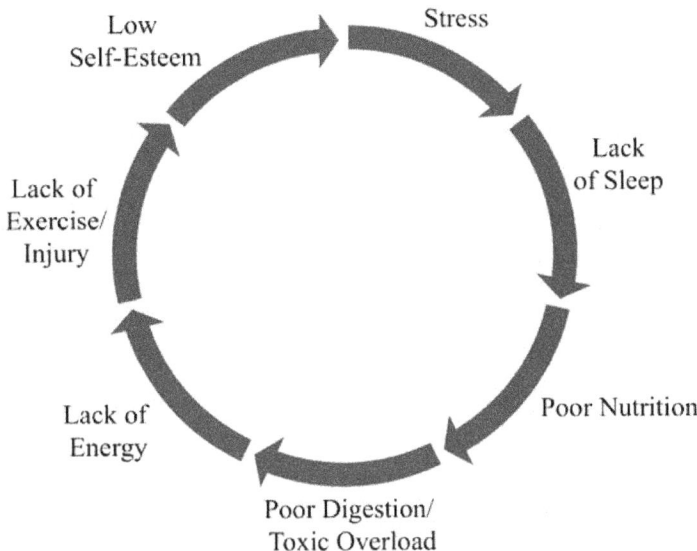

At this time, I'd like to share The Unhealthy Body Cycle with you. There is a lot of information, but I've tried to keep it as simple as possible to give you a brief overview of how the body works. So stay with me, okay? And if you like visual tools as much as I do, I hope you'll appreciate this diagram I've created to help walk you through this cycle.

Here we go.

The Unhealthy Body Cycle is a chain of events that ultimately lead to an unhealthy state. Typically, the cycle (or wheel) begins with having too much stress in your life, but any of the spokes can trigger the start of the spin cycle. As you can see from the diagram, there is no end to the circle. It continues and repeats for as long as you're in The Unhealthy Body Cycle. I'll start with stress as the first spoke in the wheel, and then I'll describe how each spoke is triggered and connected to the next.

Stress

What exactly is stress? The term *stress* was coined in the 1950s by Dr. Hans Selye, a pioneer in the field of endocrinology. He defined stress as the body's response to a demand for change. The stress response is a complex set of hormonal and biochemical signals and responses that generally affect the entire body. The kind of stress I'm talking about is any physical, chemical, or emotional factors that can cause mental or bodily tension or harm—in other words, negative stress. Keep in mind that not all stress is bad. Positive stress can make our senses hyperacute and allow us to respond to stress appropriately.

Stressors can include either positive or negative life events—marriage, divorce, a new baby, death, a new job, getting fired, moving, home renovations—that require you to adapt to changes in your life. Negative stress results when pressures, challenges, or demands in life exceed your coping abilities. Stress can manifest itself in physical, emotional, or behavioral symptoms (Chu et al. 2024). To begin to understand how stress manifests in the body, we first need to understand how the three stages of stress[2] are connected.

> *Negative stress results when pressures, challenges, or demands in life exceed your coping abilities.*

First Stage: Alarm. In this stage, our sympathetic nervous system is activated and produces an emergency signal that is sent to the brain. The body gets more energy by releasing the hormones adrenaline, noradrenaline, and cortisol into the bloodstream. Heavy breathing, a faster heart rate, sweating, and high blood pressure accompany it. Our appetite is temporarily put on hold. Blood is shunted away from the digestive tract and redirected into muscles and

---

[2] The three stages of stress are also known as General Adaptation Syndrome (Selye 1950).

limbs. That is what we call the fight-or-flight response. When we feel potentially threatened, our body automatically reacts by preparing itself to either fight to protect ourselves or flight to run for our lives. You've probably heard of the often-used scenario of running away from danger, like the tiger chasing after you in the wild. The fight-or-flight response is what helps you run like a deer (yes, they can outrun tigers).[3] Once you're safe, elevated cortisol levels return to normal.

But in day-to-day life, this type of stress is very common in circumstances such as having a deadline to meet for an assignment. Your boss delegates the project and asks you to complete it in three days. As you review the work ahead, you realize that in order to get it done on time, you have to put every waking minute into accomplishing the task. As your heart rate increases, you dial in and get laser-focused. Everything else becomes secondary to this one project. You work through your lunch break, power through the afternoon with caffeine, and work well past your regular quitting time. You don't get much sleep but seem to have a ton of energy. And even though your nutrition has been atrocious, you've even lost a couple of pounds. At last you complete your project and need the entire weekend to recuperate. By Monday, you're back to normal.

Second Stage: Resistance. In the second stage, a reduction in your energy level takes place, making you feel exhausted, anxious, and forgetful. Why? Because our stress response was not designed to deal with the stressors of everyday life in the long term. So our cortisol levels remain elevated at times when they should normally decline. In this prolonged stage of stress, people are apt to experience the onset of an unhealthy body (Chu et al. 2024).

---

[3] Deer can outrun tigers, but most of the time, the tiger catches the deer because it comes too close before the deer notices the tiger (according to a documentary I saw on the Nature Channel).

In day-to-day life, let's just say that as soon as you hand in your last project, your boss assigns you another one, and another one, and another one, each with deadlines nearly impossible to manage. Your aging parent also needs care, and your children need help with their homework and after-school activities. Your debt is piling up, and you're constantly at odds with your spouse. There just doesn't seem to be any relief in sight, and you're constantly running behind.

During the First Stage of stress (in temporary stressful episodes), adrenalin kicks in and taps into your fat stores to provide energy to fuel the fight-or-flight response. Remember the temporary weight loss you experienced when you needed to complete that one project? You can thank the hormone adrenaline for that. However, cortisol seeks muscle proteins for fuel during prolonged periods of intense stress (as in the second stage: resistance). Over time, this attack on muscle protein destroys metabolically active muscle tissue—tissue that we need to boost metabolism and energy more efficiently (Thau, Gandhi, and Sharma 2023). This essentially means that it is in the second stage of stress (resistance) when you are no longer losing that initial weight; you are gaining it instead. Study after study shows that stress causes abdominal fat, even in otherwise thin people. That is because the hormone cortisol, secreted by the adrenal glands when you experience stress, affects fat distribution by causing visceral fat to be stored centrally, around the organs. Research has shown that physical or emotional stress increases food intake high in sugar, fat, or both.[4]

Third Stage: Exhaustion. In this stage, you are completely drained of all energy and just plain exhausted. You have no motivation to

---

[4] According to an American Psychological Association survey ("Why Stress Causes People to Overeat" 2021). Read more at https://www.health.harvard.edu/staying-healthy/why-stress-causes-people-to-overeat.

work, carry on with errands, or enjoy life. This stage is a breakdown of your mental and physical system, which can have severe consequences such as increased blood pressure, ulcers, heart disease, cancer, and eventually death (Chu et al. 2024). At this stage of stress, you can no longer ignore that you have a serious health problem.

When I refer to stress in The Unhealthy Body Cycle, I am referring to the type of stress you experience in the second stage: resistance (chronic stress). It is most concerning because we can live with chronic stress for a long time without realizing it's a problem, especially because we have found so many ways to mask or ignore our body's sign language (symptoms). Anxiety medication, sleeping pills, over-the-counter drugs for aches and pains, caffeine, alcohol, sugar, and recently legalized marijuana all contribute to how we self-medicate. But the fact is that we need to change how we cope with stress. When we subject our body to chronic stress, it triggers the next spoke of the cycle: lack of sleep or poor sleep quality.

Lack of Sleep or Poor Sleep Quality

When I first started writing this book (eons ago), there weren't as many books about sleep as there are now. Back then, most people agreed that sleep was important, but the correlation between sleep and weight loss wasn't as accepted as it is today. In fact, I often heard the expression "I'll sleep later," especially among younger people. Time and time again, clients complained about gaining weight and often looked puzzled when I asked them how much they slept at night. They found it hard to believe that sleep deprivation contributed to their weight struggles. And here's why.

Sleep is not a luxury, although sometimes in a dreamy, comfy bed it can sure feel that way. But all smiles aside, it is a necessary physiological function that keeps you alive. Lack of sleep not only throws your hormones out of whack but is harmful to the overall function of your brain by affecting your focus, concentration, and ability to think clearly. Your body repairs itself during the hours you sleep by replenishing vital organs and tissues. Not getting enough sleep in the long term can have detrimental effects on your mental and physical health as well as your overall ability to function optimally.

During deep sleep, your brain secretes a large amount of growth hormone that tells your body how to break down fat or fuel. If you don't get enough sleep, there won't be enough growth hormone to break down the fat that results when you take in extra calories (Kim, Jeong, and Hong 2015). Instead, your body takes a shortcut and packs the added fat away to your thighs, belly, or butt—wherever you tend to gain weight.

In addition, the effects of leptin, a hormone that tells your brain when you are full (satiated) and signals when the body can break down fuel, is decreased by lack of sleep. In other words, when leptin decreases, it signals the body that you don't have enough energy, which stimulates hunger even though you don't actually need food. Consequently, the hormone that stimulates hunger, called ghrelin, does the exact opposite of leptin. Without sufficient sleep, your body ends up with too much ghrelin, causing you to eat even when you're not hungry. It also stops burning calories because it thinks there's a shortage. Ghrelin levels increase during times of stress. When you get enough sleep, your leptin levels should increase (tell the body when it's full to burn unneeded calories), and your ghrelin levels should decrease so you don't unnecessarily reach for more food (van Egmond et al. 2022). The bottom line is that lack of sleep messes with your hormones and does the exact opposite of what you really want when you are trying to lose weight. It starts packing it on.

Sadly, I had many clients who truly wanted to get more sleep but were plagued with worrisome, sleepless nights. They'd go to bed early only to suffer from either not being able to fall asleep or constantly waking up for one reason or another. Most times, a lack of good quality sleep was stress-related, but sometimes it was for reasons such as peri/menopausal symptoms (we'll cover those briefly in Chapter 7) or a loud, snoring husband. Either way, when you lack the proper amount of sleep or lack good quality sleep, it triggers the next spoke of The Unhealthy Body Cycle: poor nutrition.

Poor Nutrition

Starting the day stressed out and tired often leads to an increased appetite for all the wrong foods (simple carbs, high sugar, high salt, trans fats, etc.) and poor meal planning. These types of foods (and caffeinated beverages) are temporary fixes for a lack of energy. We consume them not necessarily because they make us feel healthy but to give into cravings or get through the day.

There are many reasons you may not be as nourished as you think. First, having poor nutrition can result from choosing foods you think are healthy but don't have high nutritional value. Prepackaged, non-organic, or genetically modified organism (GMO) foods are examples. Consumers must be extra vigilant in checking food labels, even when they claim to be dairy-free, fat-free, or gluten-free. They're often packed with loads of sugar or added ingredients that cause a whole slew of other problems. Unfortunately, our meal planning (or lack of it) is often directly related to our ability to effectively manage time, stress, and priorities. In fact, it's one of the top reasons people have a poor diet in the first place. Whether they have no time to prepare food, grocery shop, or take the time to eat slowly (which affects optimal digestion), when meals are not planned ahead of time, they are often chosen and consumed for all the wrong reasons.

The deadly combination of stress, lack of sleep, and poor nutrition throws your hormones off track, resulting in a constant state of blood-sugar-level stress. That happens because the hormones responsible for regulating our blood sugar levels (insulin and glucagon) are disrupted, similarly to how leptin and ghrelin are disrupted when we don't sleep enough. And over time, our body just doesn't know what to do anymore.

Here's how this plays out. Insulin is a hormone secreted by the pancreas in response to eating food. Its job is to send glucose out of the blood and into the tissue cells for use as energy. When excess glucose remains in the blood, insulin levels stay high. Chronically elevated insulin causes both fat and inflammation in the body. When insulin levels are high, the body not only stores extra calories as fat but also tends to refrain from burning it. Insulin not only regulates blood sugar levels but also triggers the biological switch that turns off the production of muscle and turns on the production of fat, particularly around the waist and belly (Rahman et al. 2021).

In order to control your weight, you must control your insulin levels. If you don't, you could end up with insulin resistance. You mean insulin resistance and chronic stress affect metabolism and fat distribution? You bet they do! Insulin resistance causes the body to overreact to carbohydrates by causing higher-than-normal insulin spikes. And people with this condition get fat faster than people who don't have insulin resistance (Wondmkun 2020). How you eat (what and when) and what foods you combine are essential to managing insulin resistance and ultimately your weight.

> *How you eat (what and when) and what foods you combine are essential to managing insulin resistance and ultimately your weight.*

Glucagon is a hormone secreted by the pancreas that raises blood glucose levels. It has the opposite effect of insulin, which lowers blood glucose levels. Without adequate glucagon levels, you will feel tired and hungry because the brain is not getting enough fuel (blood sugar) (Rahman et al. 2021). It is important to balance glucagon and insulin to maintain healthy blood sugar levels by choosing nourishing and energizing foods—natural, live, good quality, whole foods.

Quick side note: While there are other hormones that can influence your weight, the ones mentioned here are the most relevant for this chapter. What is the key takeaway? You want to work *with* your hormones, not against them.

Generally, I believe most people do want to eat healthy, but sometimes they don't recognize the long-term effects of poor nutrition choices until one day when their pants don't fit. Over time, poor nutrition triggers the next spoke in The Unhealthy Body Cycle, which leads to poor digestion and toxic overload.

Poor Digestion and Toxic Overload

We know that chronic stress and poor sleeping habits lead to poor nutrition. But it is the combination of these that leads to poor digestion. When our digestion is compromised—sluggish (constipated), irritated (diarrhea or irritable bowel syndrome), bloated, gassy, just to name a few—toxins and inflammation begin to accumulate in the body. Inflammation is the response from the immune system that occurs when something damages our cells. One reason that happens is because when we continually ingest foods that irritate our digestive tract (gut), we develop a syndrome known as leaky gut. Leaky gut occurs when your digestive tract is repeatedly aggravated by harmful bacteria, toxins, parasites, allergies, yeast, and certain medications. When this happens, the intestinal wall becomes hyperpermeable, and substances such as undigested food or foreign proteins leak through the gut lining into the bloodstream and initiate an immune response. Therefore, changes in our gut permeability not only affect the presence of healthy intestinal bacteria in our gut but also lead to inflammation and toxins circulating in our body (Aleman, Moncada, and Aryana 2023).

Toxins coupled with poor nutrition choices make it extra difficult for the digestive system and our organs to work efficiently. One of the key organs responsible for clearing out toxins is the liver. We can overburden the liver with lifestyle choices we don't think are such a big deal, but they are. Your liver filters the blood coming from your digestive tract before passing it to the rest of the body. It also detoxifies chemicals and metabolizes drugs—the stuff people take to self-medicate during times of stress such as sugar, caffeine, alcohol, nicotine, drugs, painkillers, and more. The liver's job is to process it and clear it out.

But that's just one organ that assists in detoxification. There are also the gallbladder, small intestine, and colon. If they're all working overtime, unable to clear out waste properly and take in vital nutrients effectively, their efficiency will be compromised, and they'll get backed up. When that happens, you're not only going to have digestive health issues such as constipation, diarrhea, irritable bowel syndrome, bloating, and gas, but you might experience a whole slew of unexplainable issues such as sudden skin problems, allergies, food sensitivities, headaches, inability to concentrate, joint issues, and yes, weight gain, just to name a few. Poor digestion and toxic overload directly influence how you feel in terms of energy abundance or lack thereof. That brings us to our next part of the cycle: lack of energy.

Lack of Energy

Having low energy is a common issue these days, isn't it? I know how hard it can be to accomplish everyday tasks when you feel too tired to even wash your hair (thank God for dry shampoo). But seriously, lack of energy results from the accumulation of events that occur in The

Unhealthy Body Cycle because of the body's compromised ability to process vital energy-giving nutrients. Sadly, when our body is depleted of energy, it's a telltale sign that something is wrong. Think about it. Your chronic stress leads to a lack of good quality sleep, which leads to poor nutrition choices, which leads to poor digestion and toxic overload. Toxins cause harm to the body and rob it of vitality and energy. Low energy levels impact all areas of your life—your mood, your ability to stay alert, your ability to focus and concentrate, your sex drive, and your stamina for physical activity. Your ability to be productive is jeopardized, and so The Unhealthy Body Cycle continues.

Lack of Exercise or Injury

I understand that not all people who are in The Unhealthy Body Cycle are inactive; I certainly wasn't one of them. But I would like to address this spoke with two scenarios. For some people, a lack of energy directly influences their ability to exercise. Without energy, exercise may seem impossible because, after all, if you're tired, how on earth are you going to exert more energy to exercise? In this case, a lack of energy means you're just not moving your body much, and it has led you to a sedentary lifestyle. On the other hand, if you're similar to how I was (someone who exercised despite low energy), carrying on with exercise can still lead to a multitude of health issues such as injury or chronic inflammation because of overuse.

I was an active person who used exercising to help cope with stress. But when your body is in a state of toxic overload, physical symptoms will eventually appear out of nowhere. Remember, your ability to focus or concentrate is affected by toxic overload and lack of energy. And all it takes is a split second to injure yourself through exercise. Poor running form can lead to knee, back, or hip pain. Tripping or rolling your ankle in Zumba class can lead to a pulled muscle or tendon. Poor concentration in weight training can cause you to space out (how many reps was that?). Overexerting yourself in spin class can lead to dizziness or shortness of breath, and so on. Whether you are physically active or sedentary, your energy level and the presence of toxins directly affect how you feel and what your body can do. Either way, if your muscle tone fails you because you are inactive or your body fails you through injury, eventually your self-esteem will be affected. That brings us to the next spoke in the cycle: low self-esteem and depression.

Low Self-Esteem and Depression

Let's face it. Sometimes we all suffer from not feeling confident. I'm certainly no exception. I'm not saying we have low self-esteem when we don't feel our best. What I am saying is that being unhappy with your health can affect how you feel about yourself. If being trapped in The Unhealthy Body Cycle has caused you to gain weight, you may feel disappointed seeing a bigger number on the scale. If being in The Unhealthy Body Cycle has made you look unhealthy, aged you prematurely, or has you wondering what happened to that healthy glowing skin and hair, chances are you don't like what you see in the mirror. In fact, you may feel depressed not knowing what to do. You may even feel overwhelmed because you realize that the stress you are experiencing is causing you to worry at night, which means you're sleeping less, waking up tired, having no energy to plan healthy meals, feeling bloated all the time, and skipping your workouts. The worst part is that you have a sneaky suspicion that there really isn't some little creature in your closet sewing your clothes tighter every night. No. You have actually put on some weight (you're covering it up by wearing baggy clothes), you're not going out as much, and you're feeling depressed. And on top of that, finally acknowledging all of this is stressing you out even more. That brings us right back to the beginning of The Unhealthy Body Cycle. And on and on it goes.

The Unhealthy Body Cycle has no end. It continues because one area of imbalance such as chronic stress affects all spokes of the wheel. It's frustrating being stuck in that vortex because the body naturally makes it difficult to break out of it. So the big question is this: Once you're in The Unhealthy Body Cycle, how do you break out of it?

Well, when I created the solution, I thought the answer was obvious—reduce your stress level, get more sleep, eat better, cleanse the body through detoxification, increase your energy, be active, and work on your self-confidence. I even created a well-thought-out system to help my clients do all these things, and I shared it with them repeatedly. But having knowledge is not the same as having wisdom.

During the time I was running my boot camp, I encountered many smart, successful, talented women. They always impressed me with how they juggled a career and a family and still attended my classes at 5:25 a.m. before heading off to work. The level of commitment they demonstrated to their exercise routine was impressive, and I felt honored to help guide them throughout their journey. One client I remember specifically was overweight when she joined my fitness program, but through exercise and additional nutritional counseling, she lost more than 50 pounds over the course of a few months. The beginning of her journey was filled with excitement and motivation. She followed the nutrition plan I created for her to a T, but when her weight loss plateaued, the struggle to maintain her diet became difficult, and she became less motivated. During one of our nutrition counseling sessions together, she confided in me that one of her previous bad habits had taken root again as she struggled with late-night snacking. When I asked her about it, she explained that she wasn't really hungry; she knew she didn't need a treat. She had learned all she needed to do to change her habits, get healthy, and eat well. But these were her exact words: "I know what I'm supposed to do. I just don't want to do it anymore."

That got me thinking. Her problem was not out of the ordinary. I have encountered many clients who worked really hard to change their habits. But then little by little the effort became too much, and the progress wasn't quick enough anymore. Dissatisfaction crept into their thoughts.

"All this effort and the scale won't budge."

"I deserve this treat."

"I've been so good this whole time."

"I can skip this workout and make it up another time."

Slowly but surely, all their good intentions fell to the wayside, and their bad habits returned with a vengeance. With all that knowledge about The Unhealthy Body Cycle and how to break out of it, why would anyone fall back into bad habits? After all, if you have the solution, why not just follow it?

I can't help but think of a particular person in the Bible named Paul because I think he could relate. He wrote, "I do not understand what I do. For what I want to do I do not do, but what I hate I do" (Rom. 7:15). In this particular circumstance, Paul was talking about sinning, but I can't help but see how similar his struggle was to those of many of my clients. It's not enough to know what you are supposed to do and just do it. Self-determination (struggling with your own strength) doesn't succeed long term. Neither does focusing on the wrong thing.

> *Self-determination (struggling with your own strength) doesn't succeed long term. Neither does focusing on the wrong thing.*

Sadly, it took me a long time to learn this when I tried to apply my own solution to the struggles I was facing as I was going through my own health crisis. As much as I knew as a health coach, that knowledge didn't make me immune to the same struggles my clients faced when they lost their drive and motivation. We all fell into the same trap of relying on our own strength and willpower to make gigantic lifestyle changes. The problem is that God designed the body to be efficient and practical. That means everything in us—our cells, organs, muscles, hormones, bones—was created with a purpose and function that operates in conjunction with one another. Look at The Unhealthy Body Cycle again. You can now clearly see how each spoke of the wheel is connected and triggered by previous events. That's because of our unique scientific design, the way God created our body to function. So if we are powerless to our physiological needs and practically helpless using our own strength and willpower, how can we even begin to attempt to break out of The Unhealthy Body Cycle? Well, my friend, I'm glad you asked. But we'll take it up in the next chapter.

Review and Key Insights to Remember

- The Unhealthy Body Cycle is a chain of events that occur and ultimately lead to a state of being unhealthy.
- Prolonged periods of intense stress (chronic stress) are usually the trigger that sets The Unhealthy Body Cycle in motion.
- Many hormones regulate the body's ability to manage stress, sleep, and energy needs. These hormones can be negatively affected by our lifestyle choices.
- Weight gain or disease results from being stuck in The Unhealthy Body Cycle.
- The physiological design of the body makes it difficult to break out of the cycle on our own.

Chapter 3

A Bloody Foot and a New Perspective

The back of my heel was throbbing as I felt all eyes staring at me from behind. The room was dead silent, and sweat was dripping from my forehead. My face felt hot, and I couldn't believe what had just happened. Then unexpectedly I heard a little girl say, "Mommy, her foot is bleeding." I swallowed and tried to focus. The instructor held the two wooden boards and asked me to kick again. With all my might, I gathered myself and aimed to kick those boards as hard as possible to break them, only to miss and strike the edges of those freshly cut, rough-edged boards again.

Blood oozed from my heel onto my taekwondo uniform, and as I stood there in shock and disbelief, I felt the pressure and embarrassment build inside of me. With my back to the audience, I could feel the weight of the room, and I felt like a failure. But what could I do? Walking away was not an option. Neither was saying "I can't." That's just not something you do when you're testing for your next belt level in front of a crowd of people who came to watch their loved ones succeed. No, I had to keep going, and no amount of pain was going to stop me. I was determined to muster up all the strength I had to break those boards, no matter what. Just then, as the instructor asked me to try again, his voice started to fade out. Everything became quiet, even though I knew he was speaking to me. But in that moment, I needed to focus on the voice inside of me instead. I needed to remember everything I had learned to prepare for that very moment. I took a deep breath and paused. Then suddenly, bam! I kicked and broke those boards in half.

Breaking boards in taekwondo is often perceived as a skill of strength, especially if you are breaking several boards or even concrete blocks (when you get to a black-belt level). The perception of the strength it takes to break them is often the most impressive to the audience. That's why it's called power breaking at a black-belt level. But here's the thing: Strength has little to do with the actual success rate of the break. Some of my strongest fellow martial artists have failed to perform the power break. It also has nothing to do with willpower. You've probably heard the expression "Where there's a will, there's a way." But perception can be a funny thing. Sometimes you need to miss a few times and even experience some pain to shift your focus from one outlook to another.

The day God asked me, "Who are you when all has been stripped away?" was the day I learned who I was in Christ. It was the start of a healing process, and I had no way of knowing what lay ahead. And I certainly didn't know how my passion for health and wellness would be revived again or how I would be invigorated to rewrite my book. But God wanted me to know who I was before He put me on the path to healing. I had to know I was a person worthy enough of love without titles or accolades. I was worthy enough because God thought I was, not because of anything I did or what anyone else thought. Finally, I was able to look at The Unhealthy Body Cycle with new clarity. Yes, there were physiological reasons for being unhealthy and overweight, but the bigger picture was revealed to me the moment I realized I was seeing The Unhealthy Body Cycle from God's perspective. And boy, it cut straight to the heart of the matter.

That's when The Unhealthy Body Cycle: Part Two was born. It revealed the hard truth of why I wasn't as healthy as I could be. And I had to take some time to sit with it, digest it, and understand all its implications.

At the beginning of the book, I mentioned that our physical health struggles result from our spiritual struggles, so this news likely doesn't come as a surprise to you. In fact, I hope that in some way you feel relief, finally understanding that there's a reason you're struggling with diet and exercise plans. But this next part, well, let's just say I'll be peeling back a few layers to really get to the core of the issues.

Now, back to my story. The Unhealthy Body Cycle: Part Two dials in on the spiritual struggle I was facing by not taking better care of my health. In short, it resulted from misaligned priorities and a lack of faith and trust in God and His promises. But to put it quite bluntly, it revealed my sin. If ever there was a time I felt convicted, this sure was it.

Isn't it funny how we can pray and pray for healing (or even weight loss) and wonder why God is not answering our prayers? I don't know about you, but when I am sick, I don't want to hear about how I may have contributed to my illness. I don't want someone telling me what I could have done better when I've gained weight. But sometimes we really do need to take responsibility for the state of health we're in. And I think that ignoring where we fall short (our sin) and making excuses is not a good way to maintain our health or grow deeper in our relationship with God. If we want to make real changes and live differently, we must humble ourselves and be open to hearing His convictions, even if it is unpleasant.

> *If we want to make real changes and live differently, we must humble ourselves and be open to hearing His convictions, even if it is unpleasant.*

The Unhealthy Body Cycle: Parts 1 & 2

With that said, have a look at the outer circle in the diagram, The Unhealthy Body Cycle: Part One. Remember how each spoke of the wheel triggers the next one, connecting them all together as they continue to gain momentum as the cycle progresses? The cycle repeats itself with no end. Now, with a new set of eyes, look at the inner circle, The Unhealthy Body Cycle: Part Two. Most importantly, don't jump to any conclusions before you read the next part.

Stress = Lack of Trust in God

In the previous chapter, we learned a lot about what stress is and the physical effects chronic stress can have on our bodies. But how exactly does chronic stress impact our spiritual health? And why is that even important? It impacts our spiritual health because of its very definition of causing us harm. Remember, some stress isn't necessarily bad. It's a much-needed response that prompts us to address challenges and threats in our lives. But it's the way we respond to stress that makes a big difference in our spiritual health. When we become overwhelmed with a difficult life circumstance, we tend to worry and become anxious. As Christians, our natural response might be to pray and give our worries to the Lord. But when our stress becomes chronic and worry and anxiety become our go-to response, we're not dealing with our stress in a way the Word of God recommends.

Jesus said in Matthew 6:25–27:

Therefore I tell you, do not worry about your life, what you will eat or drink; or about your body, what you will wear. Is not life more than food, and the body more than clothes? Look at the birds of the air; they do not sow or reap or store away in barns, and yet your heavenly Father feeds them. Are you not much more valuable than they? Can any one of you by worrying add a single hour to your life?

What Jesus is saying in this passage is that we shouldn't worry because God promises He'll meet our needs. But it's easy to read that passage and dismiss it, perhaps because you've read it a million times. Or maybe you're even like me and think, *I know the Bible says I'm not supposed to worry, but sometimes I just can't help it.* I get it. It kind of goes back to what my client said in the previous chapter: "I know what I'm supposed to do." We just change the ending. But here's the thing. Worry can damage our health (chronic stress), disrupt our productivity (lack of energy), consume our thoughts (lack of rest), and ultimately reduce our ability to trust in God (lack of faith). Reading what Jesus said when you're all stressed out might not seem comforting. It might even sound like something you don't want to hear in the moment. But I don't think Jesus was trying to sound like a know-it-all. He was genuinely trying to help us because He knows the damaging effects that worry causes in our lives.

I think we can all admit that sometimes we have worried far more than we should. After all, it's easy to say, "You shouldn't worry because the Bible says so," but we do need to acknowledge that sometimes our worry can become all-consuming, even when we try our absolute best not to. I've been through seasons in my life when I've gone to bed praying and found myself waking up in the middle of the night in a state of panic. Desperately I resort back to prayer but with an inability to focus, and my prayers give way to my racing mind.

Willpower! Where there's a will, there's a way.
I had the deepest desire to stop worrying.
Willpower! Where there's a will, there's a way.
I prayed and prayed and prayed and prayed.
Willpower! Where there's a will, there's a way.

But sometimes, worry does not go away, even with all the willpower we feel we have. So maybe we need to shift our perspective and ask ourselves, "Who's will has the power?"

Overcoming worry requires trusting in God to meet all our actual needs, not necessarily our desires. I think what happens with me is that when I'm worried, it's because I want a certain situation to go my way, and I'm afraid of what will happen if it doesn't. Chronic worrying breeds fear and makes it difficult to trust God. How about you? If you dig deep enough, what aren't you trusting God with?

> *Overcoming worry requires trusting in God to meet all our actual needs, not necessarily our desires.*

What's worse is that chronic stress (worry, anxiety, feeling overwhelmed) can lead to burnout. But burnout can also be caused by a lack of self-care. We may sacrifice sleep and nutrition, overextend our schedules, and even neglect our needs in other ways. We're getting burned out trying to do too much on our own. Simply put, burnout results from too much self-reliance and not enough God-dependence. We often think we need to take control of a situation and figure things out ourselves—you know, just in case. But God deeply desires us to trust Him by faith, by pursuing Him despite how we feel during the unknown, and to surrender control to Him. It's not always easy to do, is it?

Ultimately, stress, worry, and anxiety result from a lack of trust and faith in God, and when we allow our stress to consume us so much that it takes our focus away from Him, it becomes sin. The Bible says, "Do not be anxious about anything, but in everything by prayer and supplication with thanksgiving let your requests be made known to God. And the peace of God, which surpasses all understanding, will guard your hearts and your minds in Christ Jesus" (Phil. 4:6–7 ESV).

God knows we're prone to worry. That's why He made a point of bringing it up in the Bible. In Matthew 6:25–34, God gives us several reasons why we shouldn't worry. The same God who created us is the same God who can be trusted with all the details of our lives. Worrying is more harmful than helpful. God does not ignore those who depend on Him. Worrying shows a lack of faith and trust in understanding God. Finally, worrying about the future keeps us from facing the real challenges God wants us to pursue. Living one day at a time keeps us from being consumed with worry.

So here's the thing. There's power in God's will. His will is for you to keep pursuing Him with all your heart, mind, soul, and strength. But when stress, worry, and anxiety are taking precedence and consuming you, it leads you to: Lack of Sleep = Lack of Rest in God.

Lack of Sleep = Lack of Rest in God

God created the concept of rest when He created us. In fact, He even created a special day that He blessed as holy and called it the Sabbath.

The word *Sabbath* is derived from the Hebrew word *Shabbat*, which means a day of rest.

There are many reasons God created the Sabbath. In biblical times when the Israelites wandered in the desert before reaching the Promised Land, God made food rain from the sky—manna (a bread-like substance) and quail. For five days a week, they were to gather just enough food for the day, but on the sixth day, they were to gather twice as much so that on the seventh day, the Sabbath, they would not worry about having food. These instructions helped the Israelites foster a dependence on trust in God for their provisions. God also knew that they'd fall apart spiritually and physically without time set aside to spend with Him. And that still rings true for us today. We weren't designed to be like machines endlessly running 24/7.

Spending time with God provides us with the rest we need to function optimally and live well. It helps us grow in our relationship with Him and shows Him that He is important to us. It is as much an act of love as it is obedience. God doesn't want us preoccupied with work, running errands, or anything that takes our focus away from Him. We honor God when we find rest in Him. And when we don't prioritize getting rest, we are essentially saying that we think other things are more important. Let me put it this way: It means everything else comes first. And that's always easy to justify, isn't it?

We live in a fast-paced world with emails sent and answers expected right away. There always seems to be something to do and no time to do it. Sure, we might have good intentions to spend more time reading the Bible or go to bed earlier, but unless we prioritize those things, they fall by the wayside.

Since we've already learned that chronic stress leads to a lack of trust and faith in God, it's time to assess how it's affecting the time we're spending with Him. As a "good" Christian, you probably know how easy it can be to go through the motions. You do your daily devotions, go to church, and maybe continue to volunteer or serve. But deep down, something is different. Maybe you can't even put your finger on it. And then, of course, there are the obvious times of spiritual drought. You know you should be reading the Bible, but you just don't feel like it. And on the odd occasion that you do, nothing is speaking to you. You go through a season of reckless abandonment. You don't mean to, but it happens. I've been there, done that.

That's how a lack of trust and faith in God leads to a lack of rest in God. The consumable energy we spend worrying about our problems and spinning our wheels trying to come up with a solution is robbing us of the peace beyond all understanding we get when we spend quality time with God. Yes, we can go through the motions. But you and I both know that quantity is not the same as quality.

So I'm asking you to look at not only the time you're spending with God but also what that time truly looks like. Do you pray your prayers absentmindedly? Are they unfinished because you fell asleep or got distracted and rushed just to get them over with? Are your prayers one-sided conversations full of a checklist of requests? Do you just keep asking for the same desired outcome or solution to your stress without taking time to listen for guidance? Are you getting frustrated with God because He's giving you the silent treatment in your time of distress?

I know this might sound unpleasant, but the truth is that when we stop pursuing God with all our heart, mind, soul, and strength, it speaks volumes about what's important to us. (Ouch! I know.) Our priorities have shifted from seeking a relationship with Him to seeking outcomes we want from Him. We're living in a frenzy consumed with worry, anxiety, and overwhelming thoughts. We can't find rest in Him because we're not listening, whether or not it's intentional. His truth can't sink in because we're not reading the Bible, or we're starting to doubt what it says. Instead, fear and discontentment creep in. We believe the insecurities. And our lack of rest (and sleep) changes our behavior. That leads us to the next spoke in the wheel: Poor Nutrition = Misaligned Priorities.

Poor Nutrition = Misaligned Priorities (Not Giving Due Care to Your Body)

When we are stressed out and lack sufficient sleep and spiritual rest, we're more likely to make poor choices about what and how we eat. Whether it's the lack of time to prepare healthy food, the lack of energy to plan a meal, or just wanting a quick fix to satisfy a craving, we don't often choose nourishing food in these circumstances. This then fails to provide us with what we need most: energy.

Food can often be misused because everyone needs to eat to sustain life. For the general population who live in countries without food scarcity, the problems lie in overabundance, gluttony, and simply put, excess. We are blessed with so much to choose from, yet we're constantly battling with food altogether. We can eat too much food (gluttony), not eat enough food (starvation), or eat food with low nutritional value. All these cause disease, make us tired, and rob us of vitality.

What does the Bible say about our eating habits or how we should nourish our bodies? "Therefore, I urge you, brothers and sisters, in view of God's mercy, to offer your bodies as a living sacrifice, holy and pleasing to God—this is your true and proper worship" (Rom. 12:1).

When you repeatedly make poor nutrition choices over a long period of time or misuse food, it no longer serves its purpose of nourishing and energizing the body. In fact, it harms it, which is the exact opposite of how God wants us to treat it. "So whether you eat or drink or whatever you do, do it all for the glory of God" (1 Cor. 10:31).

Caring for our body is what God wants us to do. Sadly, when we are not focused on the right things in life, poor nutrition habits result from misaligned priorities and lead to sin. I realize you might think this sounds over the top. How can a few poor nutrition choices be sinful? You're right. In and of themselves, they're not. But you'll soon find out what happens.

Poor Digestion or Toxic Overload = Too Much Sin

Just as poor digestion and excessive toxins result from poor nutrition, toxic overload results from unrepented sin. Let's compare. When the body becomes "toxic," we can experience symptoms such as poor concentration, skin conditions, chronic constipation or diarrhea, mood swings, joint pain, and weight gain, just to name a few. We experience symptoms that might not necessarily relate to poor digestion or excess toxins. That's because a lot has to happen beforehand for the body to become overburdened with toxins. Generally, a healthy body can withstand a few poor nutrition choices without immediately becoming toxic. It's when we subject our bodies to chronic stress, lack of sleep, and poor nutrition choices repeatedly that our organs become overburdened with trying to clear toxins and waste from the body. Toxic overload happens over a period of time. It could be months or even years.

Just as it's possible to sin repeatedly without immediate or noticeable consequence, these sins can accumulate and grow if we are not taking the time to read God's Word, hear His convictions, and change our ways (repent). In other words, some choices you make might not start out as sins, but they could be the beginning of a detriment to your health if you are not on guard. One example might be eating ice cream. There's no harm in that, right?

Who doesn't love a little Ben & Jerry's? The problem is when the ice cream leads to a sugar addiction or an eating disorder that's controlling the way you eat, think, and behave—particularly if you become a slave to Ben & Jerry's.

You get it, don't you? I'm not necessarily just talking about ice cream. Look at the foods or habits you just can't do without. Ask yourself what would happen if you had to give one of them up for a day, a week, a month, or a year. The sweets, the wine, the cheese, the phone, Instagram, that certain show on Netflix—am I striking a nerve yet?

Similarly, sins you may think are little could lead you down the wrong path of sinning more frequently until you become somewhat indifferent to the sin you are committing. A little sin can be the first step in turning away from God, and the ones we minimize can cause the most trouble. Or perhaps you're just unaware of a sin, so you keep doing it. That's why studying God's Word is so vital to our health and our lives.

The bigger problem is whether you are physically toxic, which leads to disease, or spiritually toxic (too much sin without repentance), which the devil loves. Why? It's because he wants you to be sick and unaware of what is truly at stake. And it's not just physical toxins I'm talking about. Too much sin can also lead to toxic mental and emotional issues that damage your spiritual health. Satan loves infiltrating the way you think with lies that justify your sin, play on your fears and insecurities, or even make you doubt or twist the Word of God.

Believing the lies Satan tells you is a sure way of keeping you in his bondage and deceiving you like he deceived Adam and Eve in the Garden of Eden. God told them not to eat from the tree of the knowledge of good and evil because if they did, they would die. But in Genesis 3:1-6, Satan causes Eve to doubt God's good intentions.

Satan tempted her with the beautiful-looking fruit and convinced her that having knowledge of good and evil was a good thing because it would make her god-like. But clearly, once she and Adam sinned, they realized Satan's deception. God told them not to eat from that tree for their own protection, not because He was trying to deny or deprive them of something.

What can we learn from this? Sometimes Satan can make sin look good, pleasant, and desirable, so we actually believe the garbage he feeds us. But if we are not careful, he can lead us away from God and make us very tox-sick. That brings us to the next spoke of the wheel: Lack of Energy and Lack of Exercise = Reliance on Self.

Lack of Energy and Lack of Exercise or Injury = Reliance on Self and Not Using the Body for Its Intended Purpose

A toxic body is unhealthy, even if you haven't yet recognized the signs. When your body isn't functioning at its best, your immune system becomes compromised, and your energy levels dip. And when we're low on energy, we often default to convenience-grabbing fast food, processed snacks, or sugary options that lack nutritional value. We lose the ability to focus, we become less motivated, and our attitude changes. On a spiritual level, a lack of energy results from the sin that has already accumulated (toxic overload). But we can also attribute it to relying on our own strength.

When we rely on our own strength instead of God's, what we're essentially doing is not trusting what He can do. We rely on ourselves to give us what we want because we're not getting it from God when we want it, or we're not getting it at all. We take matters into our own hands, which exhausts us even more. God must be involved in every area of our lives. We can't separate our spiritual life from everything else, not even our energy.

Similarly, when we lack the energy to be physically active, we are not utilizing the very gift God has given us—our physical bodies. And guess what? God cares about our bodies. In fact, they're very important to Him or He wouldn't have made us physical beings. Instead, He could have just created us as spiritual blobs floating around the earth. (No need for a pedicure, I suppose.) But God had a plan for our bodies from the beginning, and we can look to Jesus as our example (Allberry 2021, 142). Just as Jesus came to earth in a body and died and came back with a new one, we will follow in His footsteps. That means that God's plan for our bodies is eternal. Our bodies are not just some temporary things we occupy while we're on earth. Our spiritual bodies are important to God, but so are our physical ones.

The Bible may not specifically say that we need to exercise, but it does tell us to present our bodies in a holy and pleasing way (Rom. 12:1). I like to think of exercise as a way to care for the body, which is pleasing to God. When we don't train our physical body in the form of exercise, our muscles atrophy, making us weak and making our joints stiff. We can lose our balance, fall, and injure ourselves. Our physical health also influences our mental, emotional, and even relational health. When we lack the energy and motivation to care for the body physically, we are not honoring the very thing God entrusted us with. (I'll talk about this a lot more in Chapter 9, Be Active.)

Misusing our body physically can also be detrimental and lead to injury. We shouldn't overuse our body, exhausting it and treating it as if it owes us something. Relying on our own strength—spiritually and physically—is exhausting, especially if our mindset is all about ourselves when our body is injured or out of energy. That in turn affects how we feel about ourselves and eventually leads us to the next spoke on our wheel: Low Self-Esteem = Lack of Identity in Christ.

Low Self-Esteem = Lack of Identity in Christ

Low self-esteem results from the accumulation of sin and the lies of the enemy that tell us we are not good enough. When we feel self-conscious, we can fall into the trap of comparing ourselves to others. Perhaps it stems from a feeling of failure or disappointment due to unmet expectations. When we feel judged by others or believe something hurtful others have said to us or about us, it can directly affect our self-confidence and diminish our self-worth. Lack of self-confidence can come from the lies Satan has told us about who we are—not thin enough, not pretty enough, not smart enough, not talented enough, not rich enough, not popular enough, not loved enough.

Just as low self-esteem can lead to depression, it also leads us right back to feeling stressed out in The Unhealthy Body Cycle: Part One. A lack of self-confidence also reveals a loss of identity in Christ. We forget that God created us intentionally and with purpose. Genesis 1:26 says we were made in God's image.[5] Knowing that we are made in His image provides us with a solid basis for self-worth. Our human worth is not based on possessions, achievements, physical attractiveness, or how many followers we have on Instagram or TikTok. Instead, it is based on our being made in the image of God, which means we can feel positive about ourselves.

Criticizing or downgrading ourselves is criticizing what God has made and the abilities He has given us. Knowing that you are a person of value and worth helps you love God and know Him personally. It allows you to contribute valuably to those around you. God made you for a purpose, and you matter to Him deeply. Relying

---

[5] Being made in God's image doesn't refer to His physical attributes. It refers to God's character attributes, and as we grow in spiritual maturity, we also grow to become more Christ-like.

on achievements or judgments of yourself or others can distort your identity and self-worth. Your identity comes from knowing Whose you are, but when you temporarily forget that, it will lead you right back to the beginning of the cycle.

Conclusion

The Unhealthy Body Cycle: Part Two reveals the spiritual battle you are in, the sin that is preventing you from becoming healthy, and the detrimental effects of neglecting your spiritual health. It's a chain of events triggered by sin that are all connected to something with much more significant consequences.

At the beginning of this chapter, I shared how people perceive power breaking in taekwondo to be an impressive form of strength as a martial artist. But if you study martial arts on a deeper level, you'll learn that it's less about strength and more about specific technique. It's about learning to shift your focus from hitting hard to hitting smart so you can apply the right technique to hit your target. Sometimes our weight gain or health issues (even a bleeding foot) prevent us from knowing what to do or who to listen to. When all we feel is our frustration, shame, and disappointment, it's hard to hear the whisper that guides us to focus on what or Who is important.

> *When all we feel is our frustration, shame, and disappointment, it's hard to hear the whisper that guides us to focus on what or Who is important.*

It's not always apparent when we are sinning, especially when we let pride get in the way. It certainly wasn't clear to me when God revealed the spiritual battle I was facing. There were so many ways I didn't realize I wasn't honoring my body with my thoughts and actions. By separating my physical health from my spiritual health, I tried to rely on my own knowledge and strength to heal myself.

I didn't put my trust in the Lord for my worries and anxieties, which resulted in chronic stress. Instead of spending time with God and being reminded of His truth, I pushed Him away when His whispers weren't making sense to me. I didn't understand the sin of overtraining and undernourishing my body to push it to limitations that would cause injury and disease. Yes, my life circumstances were horrible. Watching people die was not in my power to change. Yet I needed to take responsibility for the decline of my health. I chose worry over wisdom. I chose self-reliance over surrender. These actions and many others led to the consequences I suffered.

My friend, I am thankful that God loved me enough to allow me to experience some pain. I'm thankful that His whispers were so persistent that I could no longer ignore them. If I wanted to heal my physical body, I had to start with healing my spiritual body and come to Him with complete humility. I'm thankful He showed me where I was falling short and loved me enough to convict me of my own selfish ways. I'm thankful He showed me how to rely on His holy power instead of my own willpower. And most importantly, I'm thankful He gave me a new perspective.

Review and Key Insights to Remember

- The Unhealthy Body Cycle: Part Two reveals the connection between your physical and spiritual health.
- Lack of trust and rest in God causes sleepless nights and misaligned priorities.
- Misaligned priorities, as well as unrepented sin, create physical, mental, and spiritual toxicity.
- The more tox-sick we become, the less we depend on God and the more we depend on ourselves.
- If we focus purely on our physical health without addressing our spiritual health, we'll stay stuck in The Unhealthy Body Cycle.

Chapter 4

Ditch the Cake but Eat Humble Pie

When I was in the eighth grade in the mid-1980s, I had short hair—the kind of short that was layered all over with bangs and looked a lot like a little boy's cut. I'd worn it that way for a few years, but eventually I decided it was time to grow it out. The problem was that I hated how it looked. My bangs were always in my eyes, and the growing layers gave me the appearance of a shaggy dog. It was too short for a ponytail, too long to look tidy, and just awkward all around. So I came up with what I believed at the time to be a brilliant plan to skip the painful growing-out stage altogether. After what felt like an eternity of begging and pleading, my mom finally agreed to let me get a perm. (Don't laugh; it was in style back then.) I was convinced that those bouncy curls would hide the uneven layers and save me from the daily struggle of styling my hair. As I sat excitedly at the salon, I imagined this beautiful-looking version of me emerging with gorgeous blonde curls that all my friends would die for. I'd walk away looking just like Olivia Newton-John in the movie *Grease*.

I sat through the horrible smell of the cold perm solution being dripped on my hair through that squeezable, plastic, look-alike condiment bottle. My head felt heavy with curlers wrapped tightly all over my head. I even felt some solution running down the back of my neck and underneath the uncomfortable robe I was wearing to protect my clothing. But none of that discomfort mattered. In just a couple of hours, it would all be worth it. There was just one teeny, tiny problem with the vision of my future self. It was completely unrealistic. The experience took a turn of events when I finally got the chance to see the results of the perm. "Nooo!" I cried. My hair looked even shorter than before. The curls were so tight that I looked like a poodle, only with ash blonde hair. How I didn't see that coming is beyond me, but hey, I was 13. I was mortified. It wasn't at all how I imagined the outcome. And unfortunately, there wasn't anything I could do about it. Immediately, I wished I'd just had the patience to let my hair grow out instead of looking for a quick-fix solution.

In terms of changing your health habits, you might be able to relate to my 1980s hair disaster experience. Often it can be frustrating to look in the mirror and not like what you see—the extra weight around the midsection or thighs, the frustration of pulling up pants that won't budge any more, or seeing a bigger number on the scale. And it's not like any of this comes as a surprise either. You know when things are getting tighter, you see you're a couple of pounds heavier, and there are more rolls than you had before. But suddenly, you've had it. You just can't take it anymore. And that's when you decide the extra weight has to come off right now—like yesterday. So you look for the easiest, quickest way to get it off—a 21-day detox, a seven-day cleanse, a four-week sugar fast, the latest and greatest celebrity-endorsed diet. Whatever you choose, it guarantees results. But much like my perm, you've come to understand that sometimes the quick fix doesn't look or feel as good as you've imagined, and it only causes more problems in the long run.

Contemplating Readiness Means Disobedience

I think we can agree that sometimes we know what we need to do, but we hesitate. We know we have some poor eating habits, but we still don't change our ways. Or we know we have some bad spending habits, but we keep on buying. You know what you should be doing (eating better, spending less), but you just don't want to do it. You presume it's going to be hard, so you keep putting it off. Or you think you can make the least number of changes possible in order to achieve that same big result. There's resistance to the work involved, so you look for a quick fix. You see, the problem with this is that God knows our heart. And He doesn't want us to do something at its bare minimum or look for the easy way. He wants us fully and completely invested, just like He is with us. Looking for a quick fix or making changes halfheartedly is just as bad as doing nothing at all because it shortchanges us so we don't receive God's intended blessing.

When I was going through my health crisis, nothing brought me back to the level of physical health I was accustomed to. Even after the Lord revealed I was in a spiritual battle, it still didn't motivate me to immediately change my behavior. I prayed for forgiveness, yes. I knew who I was in Christ, yes. I knew that physical health and spiritual health could not be separated, yes. But I dreaded the thought of having to do all the work involved in getting healthy again. It would take so much energy to get myself back on track, and honestly, I was already exhausted.

But resistance to change can be exactly what's standing in the way of reaching your health and weight loss goals. I mean, after all, why do we resist? Do we resist because it means breaking habits we're accustomed to, habits we might even enjoy? Is it because it involves work and effort that might make us feel uncomfortable? Ultimately, is resistance to change seeded by our subconscious mind believing we might fail? Whatever my reasons were, I wasn't fully invested in changing my ways. I held back in obedience but still longed for a breakthrough.

Throughout my health crisis, I experienced intense joint pain and relentless achiness. Even simple, everyday tasks became a struggle. Washing my long hair was difficult. I could only lift one arm above my head. Getting in and out of a car felt like a major effort, thanks to the bursitis in my hips. Sleeping was no relief either; I couldn't lie comfortably on either side because my left shoulder and right hip throbbed in unison. The list was endless. Physical therapy and yoga improved my mobility in small increments, but progress was unpredictable. Some days I ached with pain; other days I felt better. I eliminated dairy and gluten from my diet, but my stomach pains did not subside. Months went by, and progress was slow. I began to feel impatient. It felt like I was making a huge effort, but was I really? What I was putting into it was exactly what I was getting out of it—little effort, little outcome.

Looking back, I honestly don't know what I was thinking—trying to outsmart God with halfhearted effort. The truth is that I knew all along what He was asking of me: complete surrender. He wanted every part of my life, not just the pieces I was comfortable handing over.

True healing meant trusting His process and His pace, not clinging to my own plan and hoping He'd bless it anyway. Deep down, I knew He was asking me to start from scratch—to be intentional, to invite Him into every step of the journey. And this journey wasn't just about easing physical pain. Yes, I believed a gut-healing diet could reduce inflammation, ease my stomach issues, and improve my mobility, but God wanted more for me. He wanted me to experience the power of the Holy Spirit for myself. If I wanted healing on the outside, I had to let God deal with what was broken on the inside.

Now it was time to walk through the valley.

It was time to decide what I truly wanted and what I was willing to do to receive it.

I hope and pray for you that you don't wait as long as I did to fully surrender yourself to the Lord and trust in His ways. Don't let another minute pass in disobedience and miss out on the amazing blessings God has prepared and has waiting for you. Honor Him with your willingness to be obedient, even if it means you don't know or understand His plan, and even if it means doing all the hard work. (By the way, it might not be as hard as you think. We've been led to believe that changing our habits is hard, but I'll show you how much easier it can be later in the book.) The truth is that you won't change until you choose to change. It's a choice. And if you want to change physically and grow spiritually, you have to break old beliefs that keep you stuck. That means realizing that if you want to change your body, it's going to require some faith and discipline in the spiritual growth department. You must put aside pride, come to God with complete humility, and acknowledge the possibility that your health struggles could result from misaligned priorities.

> *If you want to change physically and grow spiritually, you have to break old beliefs that keep you stuck.*

When difficult life circumstances come your way, you get so consumed with problems that your focus turns from trusting God with them to coping with difficulties through unhealthy behaviors.

Your priorities shift and cause you to spend less time taking care of your health needs and more time worrying about whatever the difficult situation is. The physical result is a body that is struggling to maintain health. Weight gain, lack of peace and rest, pain and inflammation, and out-of-control eating and drinking habits are just a few examples. You know The Unhealthy Body Cycle: Part One. If you're unhappy with your physical appearance and it's all you focus on, you're missing a tremendous opportunity for spiritual growth and healing.

On the other hand, maybe your faith life is strong. Maybe you're consistent in your spiritual disciplines, your prayer life is active, and your passion for God runs deep. You're on fire for Him. But there's this one area that still feels like a struggle: your health and weight. Why do you think that is? Are those two areas as separate as they seem? I've come to believe we're never truly done growing. God keeps shaping and refining us our whole lives. So here's something to consider: What if this physical struggle is actually an invitation, an opportunity to become even more like Christ?

I realize this may not be easy to read or hear. My hope and prayer for you as I write these words is that they will move you toward desiring a deeper understanding of God and His love for you, and moving toward a closer relationship with Him. James 4:10 says, "Humble yourselves before the Lord, and he will lift you up."

Let's stop looking for the quick fixes in our lives. Let's stop resisting change because we think it's going to be hard. It doesn't have to be. You just need to make the decision to change and commit to it. Start the process of doing the work and believe change is happening with every step you take. Sweet friend, I believe in you. You can do it. God is waiting for you to take action, and when you do, I promise He'll be there for you, giving you the strength and endurance you need to persevere. The Bible says, "For God is working in you, giving you the desire and the power to do what pleases him" (Phil. 2:13 NLT).

But before we address your physical health, let's start by addressing your heart. In the diagram below, you'll see a step-by-step plan of how you'll begin building a new, healthy lifestyle foundation from the ground up. You'll start with Steps 1-3 right now. As you read the rest of the book and begin to implement what you have learned, you will automatically move on to Steps 4-6. Here we go.

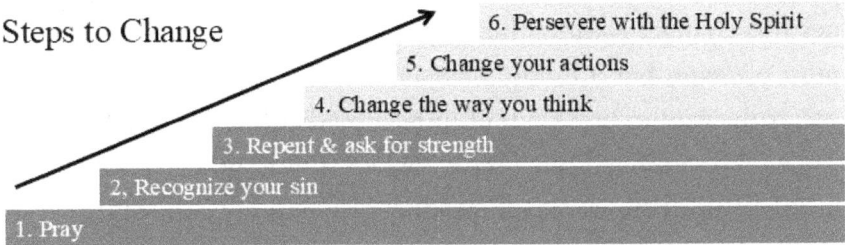

Step 1: Pray

God wants us to communicate with Him. When we come to Him openly and honestly, expressing how we feel or talking to Him about what's on our mind, we're exercising our faith and belief that He cares about us and the details of our lives. God doesn't care how polished your prayer is, especially not for the purpose of what we're about to do. Sometimes I've gotten in my own way of prayer, like thinking, "Oh wait, I'm supposed to thank God first, then pray for others, and at the end, let my request be known." (Have you ever taken a class on how to pray? I have. It was great, but don't let overthinking get in your way of talking openly.) God wants to hear what you have to say, and since He already knows what you're going to pray, you don't have to worry about the order or if you're doing it right. Some of my most sincere prayers were like the conversations I've had with myself. "I feel like a failure. I feel fat. Will I ever stop struggling with this?" Talk to Him openly and be genuine. Lay it all out. He will listen.

Step 2: Recognize Your Sin

Sometimes self-deception makes it difficult to recognize or confess our sin. If we never identify our sin and replace it with truth, our own thoughts become louder than God's whispers. Ask the Lord to help you recognize your sin and reveal which health habits or behaviors you need to change. I know this step isn't the most pleasant, but it is absolutely crucial if you truly want to break out of unhealthy diet-lifestyle bondage.

> *If we never identify our sin and replace it with truth, our own thoughts become louder than God's whispers.*

As I mentioned previously, when I was going through my health crisis, there were circumstances beyond my control that were extremely stressful for me. But I had to accept responsibility for my part in becoming unhealthy. Do that by taking an honest look at how you live, your choices, and what influences your decisions. Are there any persistent thoughts or whispers you just can't get out of your head or heart? Are there any gut feelings leading you to think that something needs to change? Look for the ones that are in line with God's truth. Don't let pride stand in the way of your relationship with God, and come to Him with complete humility. He's waiting for you with love and compassion.

Step 3: Repent and Ask for Strength

Thank God for showing you where you have fallen short, and ask Him for forgiveness. When God reveals the things we likely don't want to accept or are possibly even ashamed of, He shows us His deep love for us. Thank Him for His grace and mercy. When we ask God to forgive us of our sins, we can be assured He has, and we can feel confident to ask for His strength so we can sincerely begin to walk in a new direction. You need His strength because resistance to change could be lurking around the corner throughout your journey. Trade your willpower for His strength to help you change your ways.

Action Step: Go get some tissues, a pen, and a piece of paper or a notebook. Grab your Bible too; you might need it. Now take a few moments to complete Steps 1–3 before you read any further.

Welcome back! I'm giving you a big hug right now.

Psalm 32, written by King David, is a wonderful expression of how joyful and relieved he felt when he received God's forgiveness. Read it and discover your own joy, knowing your sins have been forgiven.

> *Blessed is the one whose transgressions are forgiven, whose sins are covered. Blessed is the one whose sin the Lord does not count against them and in whose spirit is no deceit. When I kept silent, my bones wasted away through my groaning all day long. For day and night your hand was heavy on me; my strength was sapped as in the heat of summer. Then I acknowledged my sin to you and did not cover up my iniquity. I said, "I will confess my transgressions to the Lord." And you forgave the guilt of my sin. Therefore let all the faithful pray to you while you may be found; surely the rising of the mighty waters will not reach them. You are my hiding place; you will protect me from trouble and surround me with songs of deliverance. I will instruct you and teach you in the way you should go; I will counsel you with my loving eye on you. Do not be like the horse or the mule, which have no understanding but must be controlled by bit and bridle or they will not come to you. Many are the woes of the wicked, but the Lord's unfailing love surrounds the one who trusts in him. Rejoice in the Lord and be glad, you righteous; sing, all you who are upright in heart!*
>
> —Ps. 32

And together let's say, "Amen!"

Step 4: Change the Way You Think

We'll talk about this in more detail in the Be Mindful and Believe chapters later in this book, but what's important to know is that all change occurs first in the mind before it occurs through your actions. When I refer to changing the way you think, I'm referring to how you think and what you believe. Negative thoughts have a way of repeating themselves. But guess what. Positive thoughts can do the same. In this book, you will learn how. You must believe that you have the ability and the power to change your health and lifestyle habits. If you don't honestly believe you can do it, you won't because what you believe influences how you behave.

This is no New Age mumbo-jumbo either. I'm not saying that thinking positively will change everything. In the Bible, the Apostle Paul said it best when he said, "Do not conform to the pattern of this world but be transformed by the renewing of your mind. Then you will be able to test and approve what God's will is—his good, pleasing and perfect will" (Rom. 12:2). That means you are capable of change because of the Holy Spirit's power to renew your thinking and transform your actions. When you go forward in this healthy lifestyle journey, you will learn to use your mind and God's Word to help you not only believe change is possible but to help you make thoughtful, wise decisions that will help propel you forward toward your goal.

> *You are capable of change because of the Holy Spirit's power to renew your thinking and transform your actions.*

Step 5: Change Your Actions (Part of Repentance, Which Means to Turn Away from Sin and Go in a New Direction)

Knowledge without action is just information. We all love to say, "If I had only known." Well, the truth is that much of the time, we do know. We just don't do it. We know that eating too much sugar is unhealthy, but we can't say no when that delicious piece of cake is sitting right in front of us. Yeah, I know exactly what happens when we don't apply our knowledge. We choose to rationalize our choices. "I'll start that diet on Monday. Just a little this once won't hurt. It's low-cal or gluten-free." Uh huh. I've been there, done that too. But let's face it. Talking about change and putting it off just makes things worse because the longer we do it, the more miserable we get. Eventually, the price of procrastination becomes too high for it to be worth it.

Ephesians 4:22–24 says it this way: "You were taught, with regard to your former way of life, to put off your old self, which is being corrupted by its deceitful desires; to be made new in the attitude of your minds; and to put on the new self, created to be like God in true righteousness and holiness." You can change your actions and put on your new self. Yes, you can. Don't overplan. Don't overthink. Take action by starting small, building success, and repeating the process. And just like those rewards stack up on your coffee app, your healthy habits will too. Only this time, the payoff is way better than a free latte.

Step 6: Persevere with the Holy Spirit

While you might be thinking, "Sure, Bianca, you make it sound so simple, but we both know it's not as easy as it sounds. You don't know what I'm struggling with." And you're right. I can't say for sure I know exactly how you feel or what you're dealing with. But I do know what I sound like when I make excuses to myself, my family, and my friends as I try to rationalize everything under the sun. It's really not about the piece of cake in front of you, is it? No, it's really not about having just one piece, this one time. It's all about developing new thought patterns with follow-through actions that work and admitting you need God's strength and intervention to move forward. You'll never succeed in the long term if you rely on your own strength and willpower. That's just too exhausting.

Right now, you're at the beginning of a journey—a journey that will lead you to where God wants you to be. "In all your ways acknowledge Him, and He will make your paths straight" (Prov. 3:6 NASB1995). It says in all your ways—including what you choose to eat, think, believe, and do. That is where the rubber hits the road. Do you want to get healthy again? I know you do. And you can with the power of the Holy Spirit. Asking for His strength is completely accessible to you because the Holy Spirit resides within you as a follower of Jesus. That means your power comes from God.

My pastor always says, "The same Holy Spirit that raised Jesus Christ from the dead is the same Holy Spirit living within you." If saying no to cake is hard for you, remember that it's not hard for God, and since He's with you, you can tap into His power anytime you need it. Think of it this way: If He can raise Jesus from the dead, He can help you say no to cake or whatever else is causing you to stumble. Pray for it and eat the humble pie instead. Jesus said it best when He said, "Watch and pray so that you will not fall into temptation. The spirit is willing, but the flesh is weak" (Matt. 26:41). Think it. Memorize it. Recite it. Believe it. Repeat it.

And no, you won't always resist temptation. Sometimes you'll eat the cake and then some. Believe in the power of the Holy Spirit to defeat and repeat, repeat, repeat.

If it were up to me, I may have just continued to resist change. Thankfully, God wanted more for me than I was initially willing to do. After praying, repenting, and changing what I believed about my health, I was able to change my actions and make better choices. It wasn't always easy to walk away from cake, worry, or the desire to control everything. In fact, in the beginning, it was tough. But when we fully submit and let God be our guide, He can be in charge of the journey. We just have to be willing to stop and listen to the whisper when the surrounding chaos is screaming for attention. That's when we have to pause and ask ourselves, "Which persistent whisper is the one I need to pay attention to?" Because, yes, God's voice can be loud and make things completely obvious to us. But from my experience, it's often His repeated whispers that I need to pay more attention to. How about you?

Review and Key Insights to Remember

- Quick-fix solutions cause more problems in the long run.
- You won't change until you choose to change. It's a choice.
- Resisting what God is asking you to do is disobedience.
- Lasting change requires a humble heart.
- Praying, recognizing your sin, and repenting are the first three things you need to do to begin the process of change.

Chapter 5

Discover The B.Losophy Way

There once was a woman who looked just like you. She sounded like you, behaved like you, and even breathed like you. One day, this woman went for a walk in the forest. Having walked through several forests in her lifetime, she began her walk highly motivated and confident, believing her experience would be rewarding. At first, she noticed the beautiful surroundings and became enticed by all the new discoveries she encountered along the path. But after a while, her mind became preoccupied as she trekked along. Lost deep in thought, she continued on the path, oblivious to her surroundings, when she suddenly tripped on a branch and fell. Upon getting up, she realized the surroundings were unfamiliar. *How could this be?* she thought. *I've come this way several times before, but for some reason, I've lost sight of where I am.*

Turning around to backtrack a few steps, she went along a different path, one that looked quite familiar, one that she thought would quickly lead her back home. After a while, she realized that this, too, was not the right way. Hours passed until she finally conceded that every path she chose led her deeper into the forest. Frustrated and upset, she realized she was lost and needed help finding her way back home. If only she had brought her phone. Surely that would have helped. Soon the sun would set, and it would be hard to find her way.

Suddenly, a firefly landed on her arm. She looked at it and admired its delicate wings. Just as she was about to touch it with her other hand, it fluttered its wings, lit up, and flew away from her. It paused long enough to get her attention and then circled around back to her and waited. The woman began to sense the firefly urging her to follow. She took a few steps forward and paused. *Am I crazy for following this firefly?* she thought. Just then, the firefly landed on her arm again. It fluttered its wings, lit up, and propelled forward. Again, the woman took a few steps forward but then hesitated and paused. *What if this is the wrong way? What if I end up even farther from home?*

Just then, the firefly stopped. It came back and landed on the woman's arm again. It fluttered its wings, lit up, and proceeded forward. Finally, the woman said, "Okay, firefly. I'll follow you. I don't know where you're going. I don't even know if this is the right way, but I'll put my trust and faith in you to lead me home." The woman followed the firefly along the paths, up and down, left and right, over and under. Suddenly, the things she had seen before looked much different in this light.

After some time had passed, the woman began to doubt her decision. *Did I make a mistake following this firefly?* she thought. *The way it is leading me is taking much longer than I expected. It's not the easiest trek through the woods. I thought I'd arrive home much sooner. But I have to admit that I've learned a lot about myself along the way. I feel stronger. I feel more confident. I feel better equipped. I had no idea I could look and feel this way. Still, if I don't finish soon, I'm afraid I'll lose the drive to keep going. Honestly, I'm not even sure what's coming next.* Finally, the firefly replied, "'For

I know the plans I have for you,'" declares the Lord, 'plans to prosper you and not to harm you, plans to give you hope and a future'" (Jer. 29:11).

At this point, you may have guessed that the woman in this story isn't just like you; she *is* you. You've come to realize that all those exhausting diet and exercise plans didn't actually get you any closer to your desired destination. They just led you to the Forest of Frustration. Don't feel bad. You did what you thought was best. But here's the good news. You no longer have to struggle with feeling lost and hopeless because now, my friend, you have the knowledge and understanding of how the body works on a physical and spiritual level. You've taken the necessary steps to begin the process of change. Now you can lean into the whispers from God as He guides you out of The Unhealthy Body Cycle and leads you on your transformation journey to a healthier body, mind, and spirit.

As we embark on this next part of the journey together, remember that just because we aren't taking any shortcuts doesn't mean that transformation will take forever. In fact, your transformation journey began the moment you started reading this book. I hope you're starting to feel excited because you are about to be empowered with even more knowledge, tools, and motivation to reach your healthy lifestyle destination. And remember, God is always right there with you along The B.Losophy Way, a healthy living lifestyle that embraces who you are and who God is shaping you to be.

What Is The B.Losophy Way?

The B.Losophy Way is based on seven healthy living principles that target your physical, mental, and spiritual health. It addresses The Unhealthy Body Cycle: Part One and Part Two, and provides you with a biblical understanding of how God can help you transform your health. The B.Losophy Way is not about being perfect or living by a set of rules you have to follow. It is not a diet or exercise plan or an everything you need to do in order to [insert your words here]. It's about becoming the best version of your healthy self continuously.

> *The B.Losophy Way is not about being perfect or living by a set of rules you have to follow.*

The B.Losophy Way aims to help you build an authentically healthy life based on the Word of God. It will help you face the truth about yourself (self-image and identity), your physical and mental health (behavior with your body and mind), and your relationship to God (sin and soul). Nothing will change permanently until you are willing to surrender and trust in Him in all aspects of your life.

Here are the seven B.Losophy principles:

- Be Healthy
- Be Active
- Be Mindful
- Be Kind
- Be Beautiful
- Believe
- Be Inspired

All seven principles when applied to one another will help transform your health from the inside out. What's unique about The B.Losophy Way is that you not only start transforming your health but also your whole life. That's because when you learn these principles, you just might find yourself inspired to share what you've learned, pursue a new passion, or finally commit to the calling God has placed in your heart. When you combine practical knowledge with biblical principles, you have a blueprint designed to forever help you on the path to whole health.

But The B.Losophy Way isn't just about reading a health book with a few neat ideas. It's packed with practical applications and doable action steps to help you begin the process of change right away. You just need to commit to taking action, no matter how small it might be.

Each B.Losophy chapter will unveil two sections: Restoring the Soul and Restoring the Body. That's where you'll find the tools and suggestions to help you transform spiritually and physically throughout the journey. Each chapter includes a prayer and a review to help let the truths you've learned sink in. Finally, imagine your excitement when an unexpected gift arrives on your doorstep. In the sections called Your Surprise Package Has Arrived, you'll find a personal gift from me to you. I pray you'll open it.

The B.Losophy Way is designed to empower you to build health habits that apply specifically to you since it is based on you as an individual. We are all human, which makes us the same, and though we may have some similar attributes, we are all unique in how God created us. How we process nutrients, cope with stress, or grow in faith is quite personal. I want to honor the fact that one particular way of doing things may not work for everyone. That's why there are several suggestions in The B.Losophy principles designed to help you find your unique way. It is up to you to decide what makes you feel the most vibrant, alive, and healthy. It is also your responsibility to take ownership of what you decide. So be encouraged by the fact that you get to design your health journey and life in a way that works best for you.

The B.Losophy Way was created to empower you to make small changes that will amount to remarkable results over time. You'll encounter mindset shifts that will

> *The B.Losophy Way was created to empower you to make small changes that will amount to remarkable results over time.*

change the way you think, leading to a change in your behavior and ultimately building a healthy lifestyle.

I realize that after all this, you might be wondering: But am I going to learn what to eat, which exercises are best for weight loss, or how I can increase my energy? Yes. You will be empowered to make wiser choices when choosing what to eat. You will learn how to choose a workout program that is best suited for you and how everything combined in this book can significantly shift your energy. One thing I can tell you right now, though, is that strict dieting contradicts The B.Losophy Way, and if that's all you're looking for, you won't find that meal plan in this book. With that said, I do not address fasting either. If you are fasting for spiritual reasons, I recommend that you do it under the supervision of a healthcare professional and possibly your pastor.

What I really want to bring to your attention about The B.Losophy Way is that no matter where you are on your health journey, you can absolutely become a new version of yourself, and it's not as hard as you might think. I realize that several past diet attempts may have you feeling skeptical. Believe me, I know exactly what it's like to go on a new diet only to plateau and then throw that meal plan out the window. I know what it's like to start a new workout routine only to get injured and have to quit. I also know what it's like to spend almost 10 years writing this book, get frustrated with the slow progress, and wonder if I'll ever be able to see the finished product in my hands. The fact that you have it in your hands means if it's possible for me, it's possible for you too. Here's why.

Shortly before I finished this book, I came across a book called *Atomic Habits* by James Clear. As you might have guessed, his book is about habits. It offers a framework for improvement based on making tiny changes to your daily habits. He writes, "The effects of small habits compound over time. For example, if you can get just 1 percent better each day, you'll end up with results that are nearly 37 times better after one year" (Clear 2018, 16).

You might think that getting 1 percent better each day won't help you lose weight fast enough. After all, you've probably done the crash diets and seen a lot more results in the first seven days than you would if you only drank more water. The slow pace of transformation makes it easy to quit, doesn't it? But hear me out. Or rather, here's what Clear says: "All big things come from small beginnings. The seed of every habit is a single, tiny decision" (Clear 2018, 22). And if these decisions lead to healthy habits, and healthy habits compound like interest, over time your progress will lead to the success of reaching your health and wellness goals.

I say all this because this book isn't about a once-in-a-lifetime transformation. It's about an ongoing process you'll work toward throughout your lifetime. Please don't get discouraged by reading that. I'm not saying you're going to struggle with your weight and health for the rest of your life. I'm also not saying you'll never have to think about it again. What I am saying is this: Don't discount the small stuff. Every action and inaction matters when followed by repeated behavior. Drinking two liters of water daily for three days might just make you pee a lot. Drinking two liters of water daily for a year might help you have better digestion, a clearer complexion, and help you lose a few pounds. John Maxwell wrote, "The secret of your success is determined by your daily agenda" (Maxwell 2023).

Each day that I showed up for myself to write this book, I was creating a habit. The habit wasn't necessarily about how much I wrote or how good it was. It was about showing up to write. And you don't need to guess how that turned out because this book in your hands is living proof of what can happen when you choose to commit to the small things.

Remember, change begins with a decision and when you take the first step. Make intentional, wise choices that line up with your goals and keep repeating them throughout your lifetime. If you want to truly succeed in changing your health, you don't need to do a huge overhaul of your whole life. All you need to do is decide what you want and let your tiny changes over time grow into something truly amazing. Are you ready? On your mark, get set, let's go!

> *Change begins with a decision and when you take the first step.*

Review and Key Insights to Remember

- The B.Losophy Way is a healthy living lifestyle that embraces who you are and who God is shaping you to be.
- The B.Losophy Way is based on seven healthy living principles that target your physical, mental, and spiritual health.
- The B.Losophy Way aims to help you build an authentically healthy life based on the Word of God.
- The B.Losophy Way was created to empower you to make daily small changes that will amount to remarkable results over time.
- The B.Losophy Way is not a diet or a once-in-a-lifetime transformation. Its about helping you become the best version of yourself continuously.

Chapter 6

Be Healthy:
Part One -- Temple Ruins

A few years ago, my husband and I went on a trip to Israel with our church. It was a typical group excursion to explore the footsteps of Jesus throughout the Holy Land. The entire experience left a profound mark on me, one I will never forget. It was as if the pages of the Bible came alive and I could jump right in and imagine what it would have been like to live through the stories back in the day. I loved exploring the beautiful countryside in Galilee, visiting various sites that Jesus traveled through, taught at, and performed miracles and healing. It felt like Jesus was right there with me as the tour guide saying, "And to the left, you'll see the sea I walked on, and to the right, the city I lived in." I could picture it in my mind as if it were yesterday. It was breathtaking topography, and I felt love, joy, peace, and serenity wash over me. But all that changed when we arrived in Jerusalem. Situated on a sprawling, hilly landscape draped with both modern architecture and sand-colored buildings, I saw Jerusalem as it was—a bustling city with remnants of a turbulent past.

Our tour guide eventually led us through the Archaeological Park near the Western Wall in the Old City. As we walked along an old, paved street, I couldn't help but notice enormous stones on either side of us. It has been said those stones were knocked down from the walls of the Temple Mount centuries ago and have been there ever since ("The Jerusalem Archaeological Park – Davidson Center" 2024). As I looked around, seeing what remained, I couldn't help but wonder what was beneath me. A deep sense of heaviness and grief enveloped me as I reflected on the history that took place so long ago. The Bible goes into tremendous detail about what King Solomon's Temple looked like, yet standing there, I couldn't picture the magnificence of such an extravagant building. Honestly, all I saw were large, dusty rocks that looked blandly ordinary. What was once the most beautiful, glorious, awe-inspiring structure was now buried deep beneath the ravages of history. Was it even possible that I could be standing on what had once been the sacred, holy dwelling place of God? Underneath all the rubble, was I standing on Temple ruins?

As I reflect on that moment, I can't help but think perhaps we treat our bodies much like temple ruins rather than the holy sites they are. Often when we're going through life stressed out, lacking rest, and choosing unhealthy foods, we're not seeing the magnificent temple where the Holy Spirit resides. It's possible that all we see is the rubble left behind from the consequences of choices we're living out in day-to-day life.

First Corinthians 6:19–20 says, "Do you not know that your bodies are temples of the Holy Spirit, who is in you, whom you have received from God? You are not your own; you were bought at a price. Therefore honor God with your bodies." You may have read that scripture and nodded your head in agreement because it sounded so familiar. It did for me too. But there's something significant about four little words that I missed for a very long time. Look at how Paul (the author of Corinthians) starts the passage—"Do you not know . . .?" Why do you think he might start off the passage with these four words? Could it be possible that he thought who he was speaking to might genuinely not know that their body was a temple for the Holy Spirit? Or perhaps he was trying to emphasize something he thought should have been obvious. My point here is that whether you already know your body is a temple for the Holy Spirit or are hearing it for the first time, I believe what we honestly struggle with in life is comprehending the concept of our body literally being a temple in the first place.

If God meant to simply convey the idea that the Holy Spirit lives within us, He could have used the word *home*, *house*, or *residence*. But choosing the word *temple* to describe where the Holy Spirit lives suggests the idea that our bodies are a sacred place in which the Holy Spirit not only lives but is worshiped, respected, and honored.

If we examine the Old Testament, we learn that before King Solomon's Temple was built, Moses and the Israelites carried around the Tabernacle (a portable tent) that represented God's dwelling place among His people. They carried the Tabernacle and the Ark of the Covenant (a sacred, portable chest) with them while they wandered through the desert. Once King Solomon's Temple was completed, it became God's permanent residence among His people, and the need to set up the Tabernacle was no longer necessary. But when Jesus died on the cross to pay for our sins, the need for a physical temple, a place to go to worship God, was replaced by God coming to us Himself. That occurs through the Holy Spirit living inside of us when we accept Jesus as our Lord and Savior (Rom. 8:9–11). God completely eradicated the need to carry around a tent or go to a specific building so we could worship Him.

So my question to you is this: Are you going somewhere to worship God each week? If so, is it possible that your view of where the temple truly is has been misplaced? Many of us show deep reverence for our church, and that's understandable. But we often forget that the church isn't the temple. You are. The church building is simply the place where you bring the temple.

So how can you tell if you've misunderstood this? Start by asking yourself the following questions:

- Do I get dressed up to go to church? If yes, why?
- Am I mindful of my language in church? If yes, why?
- Am I mindful of my behavior in church? If yes, why?

If you care about the way you look, speak, and behave in church, it likely reflects a deep appreciation, respect, or reverence for that beloved space, and rightly so. But Scripture reminds us not to forget where the Holy Spirit truly dwells—in us. Our bodies are the temple of the living God. Just imagine how your perspective might shift if you fully embraced that truth. How might that deeper understanding influence the way you care for your health—physically, mentally, emotionally, and spiritually? "Therefore, I urge you, brothers and sisters, in view of God's mercy, to offer your bodies as a living sacrifice, holy and pleasing to God—this is your true and proper worship" (Rom. 12:1).

Our bodies are a sacred place where everything we do affects the way we worship, honor, and glorify God. And though we might be very well-versed in Scripture, living it out doesn't always come naturally. Be Healthy addresses the three most common ways we can neglect treating our body as the sacred temple that it is—(1) having too much stress in our lives, (2) not getting enough sleep and rest, and (3) having poor nutritional habits.

Too Much Stress

We learned in Chapter 3 that being stressed out is caused by worry, anxiety, and feeling overwhelmed. These emotions are often fueled by discontentment with our circumstances or a buildup of internal pressure that climaxes when we realize we can't do it all. Stress derails our relationship with God because it causes us to look more at ourselves and our issues than to the Lord for His provision and faithfulness. At the heart level, stress results from our lack of trust in God and His sovereignty over our lives. So how can we begin to deal with stress from a biblical perspective, and how does this play out in real life?

Restoring the Soul

We must realize that a biblical response to stress is one that fosters dependence on God, not ourselves. We can do that by stopping what we are doing and noticing what we feel when life's pressures get out of hand. The first step is taking a moment to catch our breath. Focus on taking a few deep breaths; it helps you become acutely aware of the physical sensations you are feeling—perhaps shortness of breath, an increased heart rate, or a mind that doesn't stop racing. These are all physical clues that something is up. Take a moment. Go to a quiet place and take a few deep breaths.

> *A biblical response to stress is one that fosters dependence on God, not ourselves.*

After you've become physically aware of what you are experiencing, you can check in with your spiritual health. Ask yourself the following questions:

- How much time am I spending with God?
- How's my prayer life?

- How much time am I spending reading my Bible?
- Do I trust God with my circumstances and my life? If yes, what behaviors am I eliciting to show my trust in God?

Whenever I have been stressed out and taken a few moments to ask myself these questions, I've become profoundly aware of the lack of time I've spent with God in His Word. I've allowed my worried mind to take over and tried harder to manage my schedule or control a situation. I've also stopped exercising or planning nutritious meals because I've been too busy. I've cut out the very things that are most important to my well-being. Not only is my physical body screaming with symptoms, but my spiritual body is suffering too. Worry, anxiety, and feeling overwhelmed should be the triggers to remind you to spend more time with God, not less. And though spending more time with Him may seem counterintuitive, especially when time management is an issue, it is the absolute thing you must do to gain perspective and stop The Unhealthy Body Cycle dead in its tracks.

Here are four simple steps you can do immediately when you notice your stress triggers.

1. **Pray.** Although God already knows our hearts, He still likes it when we communicate with Him. He loves us and wants us to unload our burdens on Him. You don't need to rationalize that things aren't that bad yet or wait until you want to pull your hair out. Pray immediately.
2. **Read your Bible.** Spend time in His Word. Whether you are looking for Scripture related specifically to your situation or you want to explore what the Bible says about worry or anxiety, they can both be good places to start. Sometimes I feel like the Holy Spirit directs me to the exact message

I need to read. But sometimes it doesn't feel that way. It's during those times that I've learned that though I may not always find the answer I'm looking for, there is comfort in seeking God. When we read Scripture about who God is, it can help shift our perspective from one of worry to one of security, knowing we have a God who loves us and is in complete control.

3. **Build faith with trust.** After getting into His Word, you must trust what it says. If the Bible says, "Do not be anxious about anything," follow through with your actions by obeying the Scriptures. Trust God and His promises. I realize this advice might seem shallow. Don't worry. The Bible says so. Though you may not be able to stop worrying for long, the sheer practice of trying will help you build those faith muscles. During this process I've found it helpful to remember all the times the Lord came through for me in the past. You can do this as well. Write them down. You might be surprised to notice just how much He has always worked things out for good or even for better in your life.

4. **Practice makes perfect.** Keep repeating these steps every time you find yourself stressed, worried, overwhelmed, or anxious. Remember, just because you may initially feel stressed out when pressures build up, that doesn't mean you won't get better at leaning into God throughout this process. Though practice may not really make perfect, it will create a habit. And this habit is one worth keeping.

Here are some scriptures to meditate on when anxiety, worry, and overwhelming thoughts are weighing you down.

Action Step: Take a picture of this chart and keep it handy on your phone.

Anxiety	Philippians 4:6–7	Do not be anxious about anything, but in every situation, by prayer and petition, with thanksgiving, present your requests to God. And the peace of God, which transcends all understanding, will guard your hearts and your minds in Christ Jesus.
Anxiety	1 Peter 5:6–7	Humble yourselves, therefore, under God's mighty hand, that he may lift you up in due time. Cast all your anxiety on him because he cares for you.
Anxiety	Psalm 94:19	When anxiety was great within me, your consolation brought me joy.
Worry	Proverbs 3:5–6	Trust in the Lord with all your heart and lean not on your own understanding; in all your ways submit to him, and he will make your paths straight.
Worry	Joshua 1:9	Have I not commanded you? Be strong and courageous. Do not be afraid; do not be discouraged, for the Lord your God will be with you wherever you go.
Worry	Psalm 55:22	Cast your cares on the Lord and he will sustain you; he will never let the righteous be shaken.
Uncertainty	Galatians 6:9	Let us not become weary in doing good, for at the proper time we will reap a harvest if we do not give up.
Uncertainty	Romans 8:28	And we know that in all things God works for the good of those who love him, who have been called according to his purpose.
Uncertainty	Isaiah 41:10	So do not fear, for I am with you; do not be dismayed, for I am your God. I will strengthen you and help you; I will uphold you with my righteous right hand.

When we're struggling, it helps to anchor ourselves in the truth of who God is. The next diagram offers a glimpse into key scriptures that reveal His heart and His character.

Action Step: Take a picture of this diagram and keep it handy on your phone.

Let's pray.

Dear Heavenly Father,

I praise you for being such a loving, gracious Father. I know I don't need to be anxious about anything because your Word says so. Yet sometimes I just can't stop worrying. Please forgive me and help me trust the truth rather than my feelings. I lift my worry, anxiety, and burdens to You, knowing that You are my Father who loves me and is in complete control. There is nothing I will ever need that You cannot provide. Help me trust in Your ways and give me the faith to do it. You are the help in times of need. I worship You, for You uphold me with your righteous hand. Thank You. In Jesus's name, amen.

Now that we know we can cast all our worries and burdens on God and that we don't need to be worried or anxious, let's look at what we can do to alleviate symptoms of stress in our lives.

Restoring the Body

Have you ever noticed how reading God's Word and praying help you feel better? That's because study after study has proved that prayer can initiate changes in our brain chemistry, in turn reducing the fight-or-flight response when we experience stress. Praying puts us in a calm and more relaxed state by slowing our heart rate, slowing our breathing rate, and reducing muscle tension. Additionally, specific prayer such as devotional prayer that focuses on adoration toward God can decrease anxiety, thereby proving beneficial for our mental health as well (Upenieks 2022).

> *Praying puts us in a calm and more relaxed state by slowing our heart rate, slowing our breathing rate, and reducing muscle tension.*

When we pray, we feel better because the act of praying targets our physical, mental, and spiritual health. So, my friend, when God tells us to pray, it's not just to communicate with Him; He's looking out for our whole health as well. "Rejoice always, pray continually, give thanks in all circumstances; for this is God's will for you in Christ Jesus" (1 Thess. 5:16–18).

Now that we have that squared away, let's take a look at some of the things that could be stressing you out.

Action Step: Get a pen and a piece of paper or a notebook and ask yourself the following questions.

- What are the primary sources of my stress (work, finances, illness, relationships, time management, uncertainty of the future, etc.)? Be specific.
- What effects does my stress have on me (mood, coping habits, weight gain or loss, appearance, etc.)?

- What effects does my stress have on my loved ones (temper, absence, irritability, forgetfulness, impatience, etc.)?
- What are my top 10 priorities in life right now? What do I value? For example, your priorities could be spending time with God, exercising daily, or getting fresh air. They could be looking after your family, volunteering, or achieving financial freedom. List only the top 10. Then rank them in order from most to least important. (Of course, they're all important, but assigning an order will help with the next question.)
- How am I spending my time? It can be helpful to track your hours for the next three to five days to discover what you are honestly doing with your time. Record everything from sleep, work, exercise, eating, social engagements, time spent with family, cleaning, watching TV, and spending time on social media or games.

Compare your list of priorities and values to how you spend your time, and then ask yourself this: Does how I spend my time honor my priorities and values? I encourage you to sit with this for a little bit. Observe. What feelings come up? Do you notice anything? I have to admit that when I say God is a priority and then I track how little time I've spent with Him, it makes me feel really convicted.

Then ask yourself this: What do I need to change to honor my priorities and values with my time? What habits must I absolutely do each day to live a life that is true to my priorities and values? When I say I want more free time but I keep making commitments that overextend me, what I say is important to me doesn't align with my actions.

When we take the time to ask ourselves these questions and pray through them with God, we gain clarity on how we can reduce stress and live a life that puts us on the right track to physical, mental, and spiritual well-being. Listen for God's wisdom and write out the plan for what you are going to do. Be as specific as possible. Write what you will do, on which day, at what time, and where. Also, write out the goal. What do you hope to accomplish with the plan? The more specific you are when you write out your plan, the greater the chance that you will follow through. Revisit your plan in four weeks. Is the plan working? If not, evaluate what you need to change and repeat the process.

The key to going through this exercise is not getting too overwhelmed with the planning. Keep it very simple, choosing only one thing to focus on. I realize that this can be tricky if you are dealing with multiple stressors. Perhaps you're working two jobs because you need the money but you're feeling guilty because you're spending less time with your family. Pray through it with God and ask Him to help you get the support you need. You can't always change your circumstances with the snap of your fingers, but you can learn the tools to help you cope with stress in a healthy, beneficial way.

Below is a list of some of my favorite stress-reducing practices. While these suggestions are not the only things you can do, I hope you'll discover something that will resonate with you. And feel free to share these suggestions with your friends and loved ones too.

- **Incorporate quiet time.** Recent studies show that incorporating quiet time into your schedule can help restore your nervous system. Some even suggest that the busier you are, the more quiet time you need.[6]
- **Listen to music.** Music can have both a stimulating and calming effect, so you need to pay attention to the kind of music that best helps you destress. It may be that you listen to different types of music for different reasons. For example, I enjoy soothing instrumental music to keep me calm, but I

---

[6] According to an article in the *Harvard Business Review* at https://hbr.org/2017/03/the-busier-you-are-the-more-you-need-quiet-time (Zorn and Marz 2017).

love upbeat stuff to get me going. And this might be a no-brainer, but avoid listening to music that annoys you.
- **Try expressive writing and journaling.** We don't always need to talk things out to feel better. If you enjoy writing, it can be a helpful tool to reduce stress and anxiety.[7]
- **Try aromatherapy.** Essential oils may be smelled in various ways (diffusers, candles, aroma sticks, etc.) or absorbed through the skin via a massage or soaking in a bath. Calming scents such as lavender, rosemary, lemongrass, and peppermint are a few of my favorites, but there are many more.
- **Have a warm bath or get a massage.** Both can decrease muscle tension.
- **Get some fresh air; go outdoors.** Whether you spend time in your yard or go for a walk in the city, the change in environment can do wonders for your mental health.
- **Spend time in nature.** Take in God's wonderful creation. Hike in the mountains, paddle in a lake, walk through a forest, swim in an ocean, have a nap at the beach, sit underneath your favorite tree, or watch the ducks swim across a pond. The options are endless.
- **Exercise, stretch, and move your body.** Being active can boost your feel-good endorphins.
- **Engage in deep-breathing exercises.** They are a great way to relax, reduce tension, and relieve stress because they help calm the nervous system and lower your heart rate and blood pressure.
- **Have a good laugh.** Genuine laughter can decrease cortisol levels, improve your mood, and increase those feel-good endorphins.[8]

---

[7] Read more about the benefits of journaling at https://www.health.harvard.edu/healthbeat/writing-about-emotions-may-ease-stress-and-trauma.
[8] Read more about how laughter can help you destress at https://www.usa.edu/blog/how-laughter-can-relieve-stress/.

- **Pray and meditate.** I talked a lot about praying already, but meditation also has many wonderful benefits. You can meditate on Scripture or listen to guided meditation. Using dedicated time to be still is a wonderful way to practice listening for God's whispers.

> *Using dedicated time to be still is a wonderful way to practice listening for God's whispers.*

Conclusion

The important thing to remember is that while stress doesn't leave us overnight, implementing just a few small changes can significantly impact how we perceive it and how we feel about it. Be patient with the process and keep showing up. Those small steps add up, just like the ones your Fitbit celebrates.

Review and Key Insights to Remember

- Be Healthy addresses the three most common ways we can neglect our temples: having too much stress, insufficient sleep and rest, and poor nutritional habits.
- A biblical response to too much stress is one that fosters dependence on God, not ourselves.
- Worry, anxiety, and feeling overwhelmed are the triggers that should remind you to spend more time with God, not less.
- When you notice your stress triggers, you can do four simple steps: pray, read the Bible, build faith with trust, and repeat the process.
- Learning how to perceive and cope with stress requires trusting God, creating a plan, and implementing daily stress reduction practices.

Your Surprise Package Has Arrived!

Let everything that has breath, praise the LORD. Praise the LORD.
—Ps. 150:6

Here's a simple, soothing deep-breathing exercise you can do anytime, anywhere. Take a few moments to focus on your breath and feel the tension melt away. Give it a try now and notice the calm it brings.

Breathe In Peace
Get into a comfortable position, either seated with a tall spine or lying down on your back. Now, place your left hand on your heart and your right hand on your belly. Begin to feel the beating of your heart and the rise and fall of your belly. Take a deep breath in, pause, and let a long breath out. Good. Do that again, but this time, you'll count (in your head) to four as you inhale, hold the breath for a second, then let it out for the count of four.

Let's begin.

Inhale for 1, 2, 3, 4. Hold. Exhale for 4, 3, 2, 1. Inhale 1, 2, 3, 4. Hold. Exhale 4, 3, 2, 1. Last time. Inhale 1, 2, 3, 4. Hold. Exhale 4, 3, 2, 1. Good. Return back to normal breathing. Now you are feeling calm, deeply relaxed, and ready to read the next chapter.

Tip: Grab your phone and record the above counting script so you can listen to it anytime with closed eyes for deeper relaxation. I also recommend doing the rounds of breath at least 5–10 times. But you'll need to extend the script a bit to accommodate your preference.

Chapter 7

Be Healthy:
Part Two -- The Wake-Up Call

O ut of the thousands of conversations I've had in my lifetime, there's really only a handful of them I can recall. Some are so profound that they've changed my life. Others have happened as recently as this morning and are like they never happened. (My memory is sometimes like a whiteboard that gets wiped clean five minutes later.) But many years ago, a seemingly unimportant conversation at a conference in California turned out to be the wake-up call I have never forgotten.

I remember complaining to a fellow personal trainer about how unproductive I felt because I was tired all the time. This was back in the day when I was waking up at 4:00 a.m. to teach boot camp and only sleeping five to six hours a night. Predictably, whenever I complained to anyone about my lack of sleep, they'd give me a sympathetic nod and say something like this: "Oh, that must be awful having to wake up so early in the morning." Naturally, I expected the same response from this gentleman. But that couldn't have been further from the truth. You see, he quite bluntly said, "Bianca, you make the decision every day to not get enough sleep. If you want to change it, do it. You're only hurting yourself." Wow! I didn't see that coming. While his words may have seemed harsh, his delivery was not. He seemed to genuinely express concern, which really struck a chord with me, even after all these years. In that moment, he made me realize that complaining about my situation wasn't getting me anywhere, and I had the ability to make a change. I was just choosing not to. That's right. It was my choice. If I wanted to become more productive, feel better, and accomplish my dreams, I had to decide to prioritize getting more sleep.

Lack of Sleep and Rest

Since we already know that God created us with the physical need for sleep in order to function properly, and we know that by not getting it we are not honoring our temples, we must make it a priority to get good, quality sleep. We must make it a point to value sleep because when we value something, it means it's important, worthy, and useful. Don't make the same mistake I did by thinking you can get away with less sleep because you have too much on your plate. That will never work because a lack of sleep will rob you of a life that the Lord has planned and is waiting for you when you begin to treat your temple as holy ground.

Restoring the Soul

Oftentimes, the amount of good quality sleep we get is closely related to our level of stress and how we cope with it. If you're not getting enough sleep because you're up at night with a mind that doesn't stop racing or worrying, go back to the previous chapter, Be Healthy: Part One – Too Much Stress. Begin by taking the necessary steps that help you address stress with God. This is the first step in learning how to conquer stress-related sleep issues. However, if you are not sleeping enough because you've found it difficult to place value on sleep, maybe some words from Psalm 127:1-2 will change your perspective: "Unless the LORD builds the house, the builders labor in vain. Unless the LORD watches over the city, the guards stand watch in vain. In vain you rise early and stay up late, toiling for food to eat—for he grants sleep to those he loves."

A couple of things to note here are that having God in our lives and making Him a priority will help with everything else we do. But what this passage also says is that while God wants us to work hard because it honors Him, He understands our need for sleep, and He wants us to get it. The point is to maintain a healthy balance. Don't work so hard that you neglect your health. But get some beauty sleep and trust He's taking care of the rest.

Let the Truth Sink In

In peace I will lie down and sleep, for you alone, LORD, make me dwell in safety.
—Ps. 4:8

My son, do not let wisdom and understanding out of your sight, preserve sound judgment and discretion; they will be life for you, an ornament to grace your neck. Then you will go on your way in safety, and your foot will not stumble. When you lie down, you will not be afraid; when you lie down, your sleep will be sweet.
—Prov. 3:21-24

What's the Difference Between Sleep and Rest?

Sleep is the act of closing your eyes and letting your body and mind take a break from your day. Rest, as defined here, means to attain spiritual refreshment to draw closer to God by seeking Him. You learned in Chapter 3 that God provided us with the Sabbath as a reminder to pause and rest from work so we could spend time with Him. It's like putting aside a night to spend with your main squeeze or a day to go visit your bestie. You set the time aside to nurture those relationships, and when you do, it feeds your soul. And it's no different with God. If we want our relationship with Him to grow, we need to put in the time. Rest in Him can bring you inner peace even when life around you feels chaotic. That's what time spent with God does. Just as getting the right amount of good quality sleep can energize you, resting in Him can do the same. Not only does He want us to find rest in Him, but He wants us to find refreshment as well. "There remains, then, a Sabbath-rest for the people of God; for anyone who enters God's rest also rests from their works, just as God did from his" (Heb. 4:9–10).

> *Rest in Him can bring you inner peace even when life around you feels chaotic.*

Spending time with God and drawing closer to Him can be done in many ways. Yes, read your Bible and pray—check and check. But if you find the flame of that fire slowly waning, it's time to assess why. Sometimes it's as simple as we're just following a routine, and it's gotten a bit monotonous. It's kind of like doing the same workout over and over again; you start to plateau because your muscles need to be challenged differently in order to grow stronger. If you want to ignite that passion for God and break the monotony of the same old, same old routine, here are some suggestions you might find helpful to fuel the fire for God (and try to choose something different from what you normally do).

- Attend a Christian event, conference, or social gathering.
- Worship by singing or playing your favorite Christian music.
- Attend a different church as a guest.
- Take a Christian study course.

- Do a Bible study (alone, in a group, or online) or teach one.
- Read a Christian book (fiction or nonfiction).
- Join a small group at church.
- Watch a Christian movie or documentary.
- Read a Christian magazine or blog.
- Listen to a Christian podcast.
- Serve in your church.
- Watch or listen to a sermon (TV, radio, YouTube).
- Talk to your pastors; seek advice, help, or counseling.
- Seek a Christian mentor.
- Talk to your friends or family about your walk with Christ and how it's going for you.

While these suggestions are not the only things you can do to stoke that fire for God and grow in your relationship with Christ, hopefully they've stirred up a desire in you to seek Him more passionately and pursue rest for your soul.

If you find yourself consistently not prioritizing rest with God, it's time to evaluate if there's a deeper underlying reason. Are you discontent? Is God not answering your prayers? Are you frustrated or mad at God? It can be hard to admit to God when you don't feel like spending time with Him. Maybe it feels like more of an obligation than a genuine desire. Or maybe you do have a deep desire to read your Bible more but you just don't know what to read to keep you engaged for more than a few minutes. Can I offer a suggestion? Call a trusted friend and confess that you're not motivated or spending much time with God. We tend to think that when we don't want to read

> *If you find yourself consistently not prioritizing rest with God, it's time to evaluate if there's a deeper underlying reason.*

the Bible, there's something wrong with us or that we're the only ones experiencing this. But God gave us friends in Christ to journey through life together and help us when we get stuck. Ecclesiastes 4:9–10 says, "Two are better than one, because they have a good return for their labor: If either of them falls down, one can help the other up. But pity anyone who falls and has no one to help them up."

I can't tell you how many times I have been encouraged when I've talked to a friend about this issue. Instead of feeling guilty and judged, I have been loved and prayed for. Whether I was reminded of a truth from Scripture, directed to a sermon to watch online, or even surprised with a Christian-living book sent to me in the mail, knowing I had a friend who had my spiritual back was priceless.

Friend, we all go through times of spiritual drought. Don't stay thirsty. Call a friend and help each other back to the living water found only in Christ Jesus. In Matthew 11:28, Jesus says, "Come to me, all you who are weary and burdened, and I will give you rest."

I pray that whatever method you choose points you back to the wisdom found in God's Word. Reading the Bible helps you know God more intimately. It provides spiritual, emotional, and practical benefits and helps you change your behavior. As with anything, creating a plan, being consistent, and having support can go a long way. But try not to think of reading your Bible as a duty or one more thing on your to-do list. Think of reading the Bible as an invitation from God, much like when your friend invites you out for a coffee. Sometimes you have all afternoon to sip that latte, and other times a quick espresso will have to do. Either way, it's energizing and time well spent.

Let's pray.

Dear Heavenly Father,

Lord, thank You for Your patience and grace. Please help me value the need for sleep and rest. Help me create a habit that will allow me to get the sleep I need so I can function better with more energy, vitality, and focus to carry out my day. Please forgive me if I have become cranky, moody, and short-tempered because of my lack of sleep and rest in You. I lift up my struggles in this area to You, knowing that You are my Father who loves me despite my challenges and weaknesses. Help me prioritize spending time with You. I want You to be who I turn to for everything because I know that when I do, You are right there with me and guiding me. I praise You and thank you for the constant work you are doing in my life. In Jesus's name, amen.

Restoring the Body

Now that we know what our soul needs, let's look at how we can nurture our physical and mental well-being with some practical tools we can do to help improve the amount and quality of sleep we get.

We've learned throughout previous chapters that stress and sleep are closely related. We've also learned why sleep is so important to function optimally. Now it's time to implement that practical wisdom. If you are serious about trying to get more sleep or improve your quality of sleep, devising a sleep improvement plan will put you on the right path to success. You don't need to do all the below suggestions at once. Pick a few that are easy to implement and test them long enough to see if they work for you.

Want to increase the hours you sleep?
Go to bed just 15–30 minutes earlier per night and gradually build up to the hours of sleep you are aiming for (ideally 7–9 hours per night). Starting with small increments will be less overwhelming and far more achievable than trying to go from five to nine hours of sleep overnight. Give yourself a period of 4–8 weeks to implement the changes.

Want to improve sleep consistency?
Put yourself on a schedule. Go to bed and wake up at the same time every day. Our bodies function with an internal clock called the circadian rhythm. It's our natural sleep-wake cycle. The more consistent your sleep habits are, the more likely you are to have a good sleep. Creating a nighttime routine can be a great way to signal the body that bedtime is coming. Give yourself adequate downtime before going to bed. That means shutting off electronics (phones, TVs, computers, laptops, e-readers, etc.) at least 1–2 hours before bedtime. Avoid stressful activities, working late, and upsetting or stimulating conversations. Have a bath, do some gentle stretching or yoga, read a relaxing book, pray, meditate, or have a calming, caffeine-free herbal tea. (There is actually a tea called Calming, made by Yogi. I love sipping on it before bed.)

Want to improve sleep quality?
1. Keep your bedroom dark and cool. Your body produces the hormone melatonin in response to darkness. Melatonin is responsible for making you feel drowsy and regulating your circadian rhythm. Exposure to light (whether natural or artificial) immediately before or during bedtime interferes with the production of melatonin and can disrupt your sleep-wake cycle (Gooley et al. 2011). Research has shown that

sleep is accompanied by a drop in body temperature. Therefore, keeping the room cooler is ideal to help you get a good night's sleep.
2. Avoid caffeine after 2:00 p.m. Caffeine is a stimulant that can trigger anxiety, making it difficult to fall asleep. Check your food labels and supplements to make sure there is no caffeine in them. Chocolate and sweets can keep you up as well.
3. Avoid alcohol within three hours of bedtime. While drinking alcohol may make you feel sleepy, alcohol keeps you out of the deep stages of sleep (explained in Chapter 2), which are important for feeling refreshed when you awaken.
4. If you have trouble falling asleep, stop exercising within three hours of bedtime; it will keep you awake. Studies show that exercising in the morning or during the day will help you fall asleep more quickly at night.
5. Give your bedroom a makeover and make it a peaceful sleeping environment. Here are some ideas. Get a new mattress, pillows, or sheets. Have a no-electronics rule for your bedroom. Invest in a traditional alarm clock. Don't use your phone. Shut off all the lights in the bedroom, hallways, and so on, and get blinds or blackout curtains for windows. Wear eye pads. Keep your room clean and clear the clutter. Clutter creates anxiety. Keep your room quiet or wear earplugs if noise is a factor. Adding lavender scents is calming. Paint your room with soothing colors.

Fun fact: I love my pillow. It's one of the most important things that affects my sleep, and without it, I've often had restless nights and woken up with a stiff neck. I love it so much that I even take it with me while traveling. Is there anything you love that helps you sleep?

6. Talk with your family if they disrupt your sleep. If you have a partner or children who keep you awake, work with them to find a solution to improve your sleeping situation. This one is tricky, I know. Try to find something that will work for everyone involved. If your partner snores, it might be worth a visit to the doctor or a sleep clinic to see if there's an underlying issue. Or try earplugs. On nights when you really need solid sleep, even a separate bed or room can make a big difference. Just be sure to talk it through with your partner because let's be honest, no one wants to wake up next to a cranky-pants first thing in the morning.
7. Avoid eating three hours before bedtime. I know this can be a challenge for many reasons. But if you eat too close to bedtime, your body will spend the time digesting food rather than doing the nightly repair work for your organs, muscles, and tissues. Not only that, it's difficult to sleep on a full stomach, especially if you sleep on your belly like I do. Let your body focus on restoration, not digestion. If you must eat, make sure the portion is small and your meal is light.

Having trouble pinpointing your sleep issues?
Keep a sleep diary for 14 days. Sometimes the problem isn't whether you get to bed early enough but rather that you wake up and can't fall back asleep. Keeping a sleep diary can help you learn more about what the issue might be, especially when you show this diary to your physician, healthcare practitioner, or counselor. Record how much time you spend sleeping. Be as detailed as you can and note wake-up times, what you were thinking, whether you were hot or cold, or if you woke up because you had to go

to the bathroom. These details can also help to pinpoint hidden causes of stress, hormonal changes, or other health issues. The more detailed you are in your diary, the more you'll learn about yourself. You can even use your smartwatch to help you track your sleep patterns.

Tender reminders for the sleep-deprived mama
Sometimes life circumstances simply make it hard—if not impossible—to get the sleep we desperately need. Maybe you're in the newborn phase and rest feels like a distant dream. People might say, "Sleep when the baby sleeps," but between the dishes, the laundry, and everything else on your mind, that's often easier said than done. Or maybe you finally get the chance to lie down, but you're too wired to fall asleep.

If that's you, please hear this: You're doing an incredible thing. Being a new mom is a beautiful blessing, but it's also exhausting. If you can, ask for help. Lean on your support system. And while this season is incredibly hard, it won't always feel this heavy. The love and care you're pouring out matters deeply, even when you feel like you're running on empty. Here are a few gentle reminders that might help.

- Sleep when you can, even if it's just rest. Don't stress if you can't fall asleep right away. Lying down with your eyes closed still gives your body a break.
- Accept help. Whether it's meals, laundry, or someone holding the baby while you nap, say yes when it's offered.
- Lower the pressure. You don't need to do everything. This season is about survival, not perfection.
- Talk to your doctor if you're struggling with postpartum anxiety or depression. You're not weak; you're human. And help is available.

Navigating the night in the midst of perimenopause or menopause
There are also seasons when sleep disruption comes from something else entirely, such as hormonal shifts. For many women, perimenopause and menopause bring very real, exhausting changes. Night sweats, hot flashes, mood swings, and weight gain can take a toll, not only on your body but on your rest and sense of well-being. One minute you're overheated, and the next you're chilled to the bone. This exhausting cycle can continue all night long. You want to rest, but your body won't let you.

If that sounds familiar, don't suffer in silence. Talk to a trusted physician or healthcare provider who understands women's hormonal health. Sometimes medication or supplements help. Sometimes it's a change in diet, routine, or stress management. Often it's a combination of things that make the difference.

While there's more to say on this subject than this chapter can hold, by no means do I want to downplay the very real challenges that come with this season of life. What you're going through matters. Your experience is valid, and it is worthy of care, compassion, and support.

I hope the earlier tips for sleep and rest give you a place to start. Most of all, I want you to know this: You're not broken; you're in transition. And even in shifting rhythms, God is with you. Keep leaning in. Keep caring for yourself with grace.

Conclusion

Sleep and rest aren't just nice-to-haves; they're essential. They affect not only your physical health but also your mental clarity, emotional resilience, and even your walk with God. When you're well-rested, you show up differently in

> *When you're well-rested, you show up differently in your relationships, your decisions, and the way you hear and respond to His whispers.*

your relationships, your decisions, and the way you hear and respond to His whispers.

You weren't created to run on empty. You were made to live fully, and rest is part of that. So give yourself permission to slow down, recharge, and let God meet you there.

Review and Key Insights to Remember

- Lack of sleep harms your body. You honor God and your body when you value sleep.
- God wants you to set aside time to spend with Him. Reading the Bible provides spiritual, emotional, and practical benefits.
- If you consistently lack the desire to spend time with God, ask a trusted friend for help.
- Improve sleeping habits by going to bed and waking up at the same time every day. Devising a sleep improvement plan can help.
- Creating a nighttime routine is a great way to signal the body that bedtime is coming.

Your Surprise Package Has Arrived!

Imagine stealing a few moments just for yourself. It's quiet. The only thing you might hear are the sounds of the mourning doves calling or the waves of the ocean rolling in. You take in a deep breath and smile. Now it's time for this comforting Golden Hour 'Latte'.[9]

Creamy Golden Hour 'Latte'
A soothing, anti-inflammatory beverage to start or end your day.

Prep Time: 5 minutes
Servings: 1

Ingredients:
1 cup homemade almond milk
1 tsp. maple syrup
½ tsp of turmeric
¼ tsp. cinnamon
Pinch of cardamom
Pinch of ginger
Pinch of black pepper

Directions:
Whisk all ingredients together in a saucepan over low to medium heat and simmer gently, approximately 2–5 minutes. Remove and pour into your favorite mug. Enjoy!
Optional: Use a milk frother and sprinkle with extra cinnamon.

---

[9] Golden Hour: I love this time of day! Golden Hour occurs just after sunrise or before sunset when the sun is low on the horizon. The light appears warmer and softer, making it perfect for beautiful photography and quiet moments marveling at God's creation.

Tip: Though you can use store-bought almond milk, believe me, this will taste much better if you make your own. It's not hard to make and doesn't require a lot of prep; you just need to plan ahead. You will need a nut milk bag and a blender to make the almond milk.

Homemade Almond Milk
Step One: Soak the almonds in plenty of water overnight. You will be ready to make the almond milk the following day.

Prep Time: 5 minutes
Servings: 4 cups

Ingredients:
1 cup of raw almonds
4 cups filtered water
1 tsp. vanilla extract
Pinch of sea salt

Directions:
Drain and rinse the almonds well. In a high-powered blender, blend the ingredients for 30–60 seconds until you can no longer see any chunks. Strain through a nut milk bag over a bowl. Keep squeezing and pressing the almond mixture to release all the almond milk. Pour into a glass container or bottle and seal airtight. Shake before each use. It can be stored in the refrigerator for 3–5 days.

Chapter 8

Be Healthy: Part Three -- Are We Just a Golgi Apparatus?

Do you remember science class? I don't know what grade I was in when we started studying biology, but I thought it was pretty cool. Learning about microscopic cells and trying to pronounce words like mitochondria, endoplasmic reticulum, and my favorite—Golgi apparatus[10]—was fun. Even as I write these super-funny-sounding words, I can't stop smiling. I found it fascinating to learn what the human body was made of—a bunch of tiny little cells that reproduce and eventually die off.

The cool thing about studying biology was learning that we don't need to worry when a few cells die because our body naturally reproduces thousands of them throughout our lifetime. So how do they reproduce? They use the nutrients we ingest through our food. That's why you may have heard the common expression, you are what you eat. And I believe to some extent that rings true. But I love the way nutritionist and writer Adelle Davis put it when she said,

---

[10] A Golgi apparatus is part of a cell. It processes a broad range of biologic molecules (Cooper 2000).

"We are indeed much more than what we eat, but what we eat can nevertheless help us to be much more than what we are" ("What She Said" 2024). Simply put, you are made up of much more than the sum of your meals (or a Golgi apparatus), but if you want to live your best life, you're going to want to eat the foods that help you thrive—foods that give you energy, vitality, strength, and yes, help fight off disease and even make the skin radiant and shine a healthy-looking glow. These types of foods are typically not prepackaged, genetically modified, or laden with high fructose corn syrup, MSG, or trans fats. They are natural, live, good-quality foods that help us look and feel more like a gorgeous apparatus.

Poor Nutrition

So here's the thing, my friend. I know in your heart you truly want to be healthy. You want to choose foods that nourish your body and help you feel your best. But I also understand how challenging it can be when life feels overwhelming and your best intentions get lost in the chaos. Believe me, I've been there more times than I can count.

You tell yourself you'll order the salad, but it's been a long, hard day, so the comfort food wins. You're behind on everything, and picking up a pizza feels like the only sane option. You're tired of feeling like everyone else can eat what they love without consequence while you just look at something indulgent and feel it on the scale.

And sometimes, to make it more confusing, we think we're eating healthy, but we're not, at least not in a way that's serving our body or our life right now. There's so much conflicting, outdated, and misleading information out there that it's hard to know what to eat, when to eat, or how to combine foods well. We might be clinging to a diet myth from our 20s that just doesn't work anymore. And it's not your fault. It's genuinely confusing.

The thing is, when we constantly reach for convenience foods—especially when they lack the nutrients our bodies need—we're missing out on what food was meant to do: fuel and nourish us. And when we start using food to cope with stress, frustration, boredom, or pain, we're asking it to solve a problem it was never meant to fix.

> *When we start using food to cope with stress, frustration, boredom, or pain, we're asking it to solve a problem it was never meant to fix.*

This isn't about perfection. God doesn't say we can't enjoy a treat or share a meal that's more about connection than nutrition. Food is a gift meant to be enjoyed, especially in community. But turning to food as a comfort instead of turning to God is where we start to get off track. God wants to be our refuge. Our spiritual nourishment comes from Him. And our physical nourishment should come from foods that help us feel alive, energetic, vibrant, and whole—not depleted, sluggish, or unwell. That's why practicing mindfulness, self-control, and discipline matters—not in a restrictive way but in a life-giving, freedom-bringing way that honors both our body and our spirit.

So how do you combat the struggle between choosing foods that nourish and choosing foods that are convenient? You must be resolved to make healthier choices. *Resolve* is a strong word. It means being devoted to a principle and committed to a course of action. It's not about momentary motivation; it's about choosing ahead of time what matters most and sticking with it, even when it takes a little more effort.

There's a guy in the Bible named Daniel who had strong resolve. I'll paraphrase the first chapter of Daniel to give you the gist of the story. Daniel was a young man who was captured (among thousands of others) and deported to Babylon after the land of Judah was conquered. King Nebuchadnezzar ordered Ashpenaz, chief of his court officials, to bring him several Israelites to be trained to serve in the palace. But the king wasn't just looking for ordinary individuals. He wanted good-looking, intelligent, well-informed men who showed an aptitude for learning and were quick to understand things. Among the chosen Israelites were Daniel and his friends.

During this time, King Nebuchadnezzar attempted to change their religious loyalty by changing their names and offering them food and wine they were likely not supposed to eat according to Jewish law. But Daniel showed a strong resolve to what he believed in and asked permission not to defile himself by eating the food the king offered. Instead, Daniel and his friends asked to be tested and compared to the other servants after 10 days of eating only vegetables and drinking water. Daniel 1:15 says, "At the end of the ten days, they looked healthier and better nourished than any of the young men who ate the royal food." Daniel 1:20 goes on to say, "In every matter of wisdom and understanding about which the king questioned them, he found them ten times better than all the magicians and enchanters in his whole kingdom."

I'm not saying you should only eat vegetables and drink water, though having more of those would be highly beneficial (and Starbucks would go out of business). But what I am saying is that when Daniel resolved not to defile himself, he was being true to a lifelong determination to do what he believed and not give in to the pressures around him.

It's easy to get off track and choose unhealthy eating habits when we let the pressures of everyday chaos overpower us. But having the resolve to make better, healthier choices means thinking through our convictions before we're in a difficult situation. That means preplanning and having a strategy. We'll get into trouble if we haven't decided beforehand where to draw the line. After all, isn't it usually when we haven't packed a lunch, haven't prepared healthy snacks, or missed a meal that we're most likely to grab whatever convenient food is on hand? I don't know about you, but when I'm starving or have had a bad day and my fridge isn't stocked, it's like a free pass to eat whatever I crave, not necessarily what's nutritious for me. Please don't misunderstand what I'm trying to say here. Of course, there are times you can absolutely enjoy a less-than-nutritious meal. Lord only knows I love pizza. But God wants us to find balance, exercise self-control, and avoid compulsions or binging. (For more on mindful eating, see Chapter 11, Be Kind.) "'Everything is permissible for me,' but not everything is beneficial. 'Everything is permissible for me,' but I will not be mastered by anything" (1 Cor. 6:12 CSB).

We should be mindful not to let the occasional poor nutrition choices balloon into lifelong bad habits. Since God gives us freedom, we should be cautious not to abuse this freedom to hurt ourselves or influence others. "They promise them freedom, while they themselves are slaves of depravity—for 'people are slaves to whatever has mastered them'" (2 Pet. 2:19). In other words, a person is a slave to whatever controls them. Christ frees us to serve Him—a freedom that results in our ultimate good.

If food is an area you're struggling with, remember The Unhealthy Body Cycle: Part One. Often we choose nutrient-depleted food because of the challenging circumstances we face. We're stressed out, we don't get enough sleep, and our hormones are out of whack. All these contribute to cravings that cause us to look for food or caffeine to boost our energy and emotions. These misaligned priorities compromise our body—our holy temple. Sure, sometimes we eat for reasons beyond just fueling our bodies. But we shouldn't abuse food as a way to fulfill other needs and emotions. We can absolutely find nourishment and enjoyment in eating food for the right reasons. If you struggle in this area, ask God to reveal to you what you are struggling with the most. Are you stressed out? Are you tired? Frustrated? Angry? Lonely? Bored? Are finances an issue? Time Management? Spend time with the Lord to get to the heart issue and ask Him to help you seek Him instead of food.

Restoring the Soul

"But Bianca, we both know that sometimes, even when we have made the plan to eat a healthier meal, we don't always feel like sticking to the plan." Friend, I hear ya. Sometimes, even when the healthy ingredients are sitting right there in the fridge waiting for you to create that nutritious meal bomb, a little temptation comes with a simple question like this: "What do you feel like eating?" And if we're tempted to give in to that temptation by basing our meals on how we're feeling, the enemy can use that emotion to hijack our best intentions and turn our would-be healthy choices into meals that cater to our fleshly desires.

So here's what you need to do. To kick temptation to the curb, you need to be prepared for Satan's schemes. Be on watch for his tricks because he doesn't just use your feelings. He'll tempt you with your eyes (the dessert shelf at the bakery), your sense of smell (the popcorn at the movie theater), an all-inclusive vacation (buffets galore), or the reward (you've worked so hard, you deserve this mindset). Thankfully, God gave us an offensive weapon to use if we take the time to prepare for the spiritual battle in advance.

> *Finally, be strong in the Lord and in his mighty power. Put on the full armor of God, so that you can take your stand against the devil's schemes. For our struggle is not against flesh and blood, but against the rulers, against the authorities, against the powers of this dark world and against the spiritual forces of evil in the heavenly realms. Therefore put on the full armor of God,*

> *so that when the day of evil comes, you may be able to stand your ground, and after you have done everything, to stand. Stand firm then, with the belt of truth buckled around your waist, with the breastplate of righteousness in place, and with your feet fitted with the readiness that comes from the gospel of peace. In addition to all this, take up the shield of faith, with which you can extinguish all the flaming arrows of the evil one. Take the helmet of salvation and the sword of the Spirit, which is the word of God. And pray in the Spirit on all occasions with all kinds of prayers and requests. With this in mind, be alert and always keep on praying for all the Lord's people.*
> —Eph. 6:10–18

We must use the sword of the Spirit (the Word of God) to conquer our enemy and his attacks. Whenever you are tempted to dismiss your healthy-eating resolve, remember that you have a choice. And sometimes, even though sticking to your getting-healthy intentions can feel hard, memorizing Scripture can have a tremendous impact on managing your physical, mental, and emotional cravings. Don't go through the trouble of preparing healthy meals and snacks, only to be defeated by the devil's pinch-points. Fight back with the weapon you know will crush his evil attempts: God's Word. Here are a few verses for you to memorize to get you started.

> *Do not work for food that spoils, but for food that endures to eternal life, which the Son of Man will give you. For on him God the Father has placed his seal of approval.*
> —John 6:27

> *Jesus answered, "It is written: 'Man shall not live on bread alone, but on every word that comes from the mouth of God.'"*
> —Matt. 4:4

Then Jesus declared, "I am the bread of life. Whoever comes to me will never go hungry, and whoever believes in me will never be thirsty."

—John 6:35

Here's one final thought. Never let Satan's attempts to derail you become the very things that keep you from seeking the Lord. None of us are perfect, and we all make choices we sometimes regret. God doesn't expect perfection. Satan just tries to make us think He does. Don't fall into the devil's trap of indulging in those unhealthy habits only to use the guilt against you to make you feel less than the beloved daughter of God that you are. So you might stumble. Big deal. Expect it. But don't stay down on the ground like the snake that slithers on his belly in the dust. He has to stay down there. But you, my friend, were made for more. Get up. Dust yourself off and shine like you were meant to shine.

> *God doesn't expect perfection. Satan just tries to make us think He does.*

Let's pray.

Dear Heavenly Father,

Lord, I praise You, for You are full of goodness and righteousness. You know every cell in my body. You know me inside out. When I need nourishment for my soul, I want to come to You. Help me prioritize my health—to have the same resolve Daniel had to resist temptation—and accept that I am flesh and not perfect. Help me forgive myself when I make poor choices, and help me not to dwell on them either. Your grace covers my faults. Your Word empowers me to overcome any situation. Lord, I thank You for Your strength and encouragement. In Jesus's name, amen.

Restoring the Body
How to Improve Nutrition Habits

In my experience, whenever one of my clients decided to start eating healthier, their first instinct was often to do a complete overhaul. By Monday, all the junk food was tossed, and the fridge, freezer, and pantry were stocked top to bottom with only healthy options—out of sight, out of mind, right? But here's the problem. This all-or-nothing approach usually triggers a subtle, subconscious shift into diet mode, even if that's not the intention. Suddenly it feels like you're on a plan with rules, and the moment you step outside those rules, the guilt creeps in.

So what's a girl to do? Keep the treats in the house and face temptation every time you open the cupboard, or toss them all out and end up feeling restricted? The answer isn't as black and white as we'd like it to be. It really comes down to how you think about food. If you see food only in categories of good or bad, you'll likely feel guilt anytime you enjoy something indulgent. But if you struggle with intense cravings, keeping certain foods around might make it harder to break unhealthy habits. That's why it's so important to start by gradually creating new, healthier rhythms, both in your habits and in your thinking.

Lasting change takes time because it's not just about what you eat; it's about how you think. You're probably working against years of learned beliefs such as "carbs are bad" or "that won't work for me." And when we dismiss small, steady steps as insignificant, we overwhelm ourselves trying to do everything at once. Do you remember what we talked about in Chapter 5? It's the small, consistent changes that really add up. Keep it simple. Keep it doable. And you'll not only make the journey easier, but you'll start seeing results that actually last.

To build healthier habits that actually stick, it's important to start with awareness. You need to know where you're beginning in order to know where to go. One of the most effective ways to do this is by keeping a food log. For the next 7–10 days (yes, include the weekend), write down everything you eat and drink. The more detailed you are, the better. This is helpful for two big reasons.

First, you might be surprised by what you notice. Most of us aren't fully aware of how much, how often, or even why we're eating until we see it written down. You may even start to see patterns such as cravings at certain times of the day. Your food choices are often tied to your mood, energy levels, circumstances, or fluctuating hormones, and recognizing those triggers can offer powerful insight.

> *Most of us aren't fully aware of how much, how often, or even why we're eating until we see it written down.*

Second, from my experience as a health coach, the simple act of tracking food makes you more intentional. Clients who knew they'd be showing their food logs to me almost always started making better choices just because they were paying closer attention. It's not about judgment. It's about becoming more aware and honest with yourself.

Once you've completed your food log, take a step back and review it with curiosity, not criticism. Where do you notice opportunities for change? What stands out? This will give you a clear starting point and a realistic, grace-filled path forward. Here are a few simple, doable habits you can begin practicing right away.

- **Drink more water.** Aim for 2–3 liters a day. Study after study has shown that most people are dehydrated. Yet this is the one tip people dismiss more than any other weight-loss suggestion because it seems so basic. The truth is, it's one of the easiest things you can do that will yield a huge return. People often mistake thirst for hunger and reach for food instead of a glass of water. That means they're eating more than they need to. Drinking more water is like building compound interest. Do it for three days, and all you'll have to do is pee a lot. Do it for a year, and you'll see and feel the visible results. Drinking more water will increase your energy, improve your skin tone, aid in digestion, and help you lose weight, just to name a few. So go ahead and chug that H_2O.

- **Prep healthy meals and snacks ahead of time.** Spend a few hours one day a week cutting up your veggies and portioning foods so they are quick and easy to prepare or take with you. Get the whole family involved and it'll get done faster. Encourage your family to not only eat healthier but to chip in so the burden doesn't fall just on you to keep the fridge stocked and containers full. Preplan meals and precook and freeze for the days you don't feel like cooking or don't have a lot of time. Save leftovers. Plan your meals and snacks in advance so you can choose your food rather than have it choose you.

- **Designate a specific place to eat your meals.** Whether at the dinner table, a lunchroom, or a park bench, when you choose to eat somewhere specifically, you choose to eat focused. Often we eat distracted if we're sitting in front of the TV or at a desk at work. Having a designated place signals the body and mind that this is where I eat, which can help us eat more mindfully. *Tip:* If you're serious about breaking the habit of eating a whole bag of chips every time you watch TV, try making that habit more inconvenient. Let's say the craving hits. Rather than grabbing the bag and heading for the couch, pause. Turn off the TV, go to the kitchen, pour a small bowl of the chips, and sit at the table to eat them. And here's the twist. Say out loud, "I'm going to eat a bowl of chips now." I know, it sounds a little ridiculous. But try it. The moment you name it, the habit shifts from automatic to intentional. That's the goal when it comes to food, making choices on purpose, not out of habit. You can also take it a step further by mentally playing it forward. Ask yourself, "How am I going to feel after I eat this?" Focus on the physical—will I feel bloated, tired, or sluggish?—instead of the emotional guilt or frustration that often follows. That quick pause can be a powerful reset. It gives you the chance to choose rather than just react.

- **Don't rush through your meal; eat slowly.** This is beneficial for two reasons. First, it can help with portion control. It takes 20 minutes for the stomach to signal to the brain that it is satiated. You'll likely overeat if you finish your meal in a fast seven minutes. Eat until you are satisfied, not necessarily full or until your plate is empty. Second, slowing down eases the digestive process. And actually, there's a third reason—so you can enjoy both the food and the company you're with. *Tip:* If you're pausing to say grace before you eat, ask God to help you make wise choices for your next meal. (Remember, Daniel prepared for temptation before the situation arose.)

- **Seek a coach and become accountable.** One of the best ways to create lasting health habits is to get support from a professional. Sure, it's cheaper and more convenient to download a meal plan from the Internet and dive into a new diet. But you probably already know how that story goes. When motivation fades and the results slow down, it's all too easy to give up. I'm not saying you have to hire a coach to see progress. After all, I wrote this book to guide and support you on your journey. But sometimes, having a coach is the very thing that keeps you moving forward instead of starting over again next Monday.

Bonus: See the back of the book for 30 Easy-to-Implement Nutrition Tips.

Conclusion

The key to changing your nutrition habits is to recognize they don't change overnight. You're going to experience some ups and downs, and that's okay. But by having the resolve to make better choices and implementing a strategy with a few subtle changes, you can and will be able to create healthy living habits that align with your priorities.

> "A committed woman learns to choose what she wants most, over what she wants now"
> —(Koziarz 2016, 7).

Review and Key Insights to Remember

- Poor nutritional habits result from misaligned priorities. Having the resolve to make better, wiser, healthier choices means thinking through your convictions before you are in a difficult situation.
- When you habitually choose food as a substitute or remedy for challenging circumstances, you are misusing food to mask a problem that food cannot solve.
- Implementing healthier habits that last requires time and patience. Avoid being overwhelmed by aiming for simple, gradual changes you can maintain consistently. Support from a coach can help.
- Temptation and setbacks are bound to come. The quicker you get over them, the better.
- "A committed woman learns to choose what she wants most, over what she wants now" (Koziarz 2016, 7).

Your Surprise Package Has Arrived!

I couldn't possibly let you read a chapter about food without sharing one of my favorite salad recipes. I've combined roasted beets, massaged kale (tastes way better that way), pistachios, and a shredded apple to give you all the nourishment and goodness in one delicious bowl. Feel free to eat it on its own or combine it with your favorite source of protein.

Roasted Beet and Pistachio Salad

Prep Time: 20 minutes (or less if you have help)
Roasting Time: 35–40 minutes
Servings: 4

Ingredients:

3 medium red beets, peeled and cut into 1-inch wedges
3 medium golden beets, peeled and cut into 1-inch wedges
½ tsp. sea salt
¼ tsp. black pepper
3 tbsp. extra virgin olive oil
1 tbsp. Italian seasoning
3 large garlic cloves, minced
¼ cup raw pistachios
1 large bunch of kale, washed and destemmed, torn into bite-sized pieces
1 medium apple, shredded

Optional:
½ cup grated fresh parmesan cheese
4 tsp. hulled hemp seeds
Nutritional yeast to taste

Dressing:
4 tbsp. extra virgin olive oil
2 tbsp. fresh lemon juice
1 tbsp. raw honey
1 tsp. apple cider vinegar
1/8 tsp. sea salt

Directions:
Preheat oven to 395°F. In a medium bowl, toss the beets with olive oil, garlic, salt, pepper, and Italian seasoning. Stir and coat well. Arrange the beets on a baking sheet and cover lightly with foil. Bake for 35–40 minutes until tender but firm. (Let sit for 15 minutes to cool before adding to salad.)

Meanwhile, toss the kale into a large bowl and pour the dressing on top. Massage the kale with your hands until the dressing is well distributed and the kale begins to soften. Add the shredded apple. Mix and set aside.

When ready to serve, place the salad in bowls, add the roasted beets, and distribute the pistachios. Garnish with parmesan cheese, or sprinkle with hemp seeds and nutritional yeast for a dairy-free option.

Chapter 9

Be Active:
Falling Down and Getting Up

Before I launched my boot camp business, I worked as a personal trainer at a high-end gym in Toronto. One of my very first clients was a successful author in her mid-50s who had recently joined the gym to get back in shape. She admitted she'd become quite sedentary after years of sitting at her desk writing. After running through the standard fitness assessments, we moved into the workout area to begin her first training session. I demonstrated each exercise, explained how to do it, and guided her through it.

Things were going smoothly until we hit a wall halfway through the session. She hesitated at the edge of the mat when I asked her to perform a basic abdominal exercise. Her face flushed with embarrassment as she looked at me and said quietly, "I can't do that." Gently, I asked, "Why not?" Her answer stopped me in my tracks. It wasn't the exercise she couldn't do; it was getting down on the floor. More specifically, she was afraid she wouldn't be able to get back up. That moment tugged at my heart. I couldn't let her leave without addressing my concern. Her fear, though tied to a small physical task, was a much bigger issue. Being able to get down on the floor and back up again wasn't just a gym movement; it was a life skill, and one she desperately needed to have.

During that session, I gently shared my concerns about her mobility. With empathy and care, I helped her see that her fear wasn't just holding her back in the gym; it was limiting her ability to live life fully. As a successful author, her livelihood depended on being able to move confidently and independently. I asked her to imagine falling while doing something simple at home and not being able to get back up, perhaps missing an important interview or media appearance. What if she tripped while walking on stage during a book event? (Remember when Jennifer Lawrence fell on the Oscar stairs in 2013?) She smiled, but the point hit home. She realized this wasn't just about core strength; it was about freedom. And her life really did depend on it.

From that day forward, we focused on building the strength, confidence, and mobility she needed, not just to get onto the floor but to rise back up with ease. Week by week her body grew stronger, her fear faded, and her confidence soared.

Training that client taught me an important lesson about why being active is so important. It isn't just about exercising to look or feel great, although that's a pleasant side effect. It helps us accomplish everyday tasks, which makes our lives easier and helps us carry out God's will.

Don't Ignore the Importance of the Physical Body

God intentionally created us with a physical body. When we don't take care of it, we become tight and stiff, and our muscles weaken. We develop aches and pains. We become out of shape, tired, and sluggish. I honestly can't tell you that there's scripture in the Bible that says, "Thou shalt exercise," but the Bible does reference that physical activity is beneficial. First Timothy 4:8 says, "For physical training is of some value, but godliness has value for all things, holding promise for both the present life and the life to come."

I suppose it's possible to read this scripture and dismiss the importance of physical training. Yes, pursuing godliness has more value than physical training, but it doesn't say that physical training has no value at all. In fact, look at some other verses from the Bible and how much exercise is referenced.

> *Do you not know that in a race all the runners run, but only one receives the prize? So run that you may obtain it. Every athlete exercises self-control in all things. They do it to receive a perishable wreath, but we an imperishable. So I do not run aimlessly; I do not box as one beating the air. But I discipline my body and keep it under control, lest after preaching to others I myself might be disqualified.*
> —1 Cor. 9:24-27 ESV

If you've studied this passage before, you may know that Paul (the author of Corinthians) is referencing how Christians should live out their lives on earth with our hope in Christ and living for the prize, which is eternal. But we shouldn't disregard what else it says.

Back in Paul's day, he was writing to people who were likely familiar with athletic competitions, much like the Olympic Games. He uses the example of athletic competition to point out that an athlete trains to win the prize, the perishable wreath. But notice what else Paul says. Only one wins the prize. So how do they obtain it? By having self-control in all things. A woman needs to know what she wants. And if she wants to win, she has to train consistently, not just every now and then. If she truly wants to win the prize, she needs to discipline herself not only through exercise but also in lifestyle choices that reflect her values. Winning the prize requires intentionality and it will only happen with commitment.

I'm not saying you need to strive to be an athlete. But there are things we can learn from athletes. They discipline their body to win the prize. We need to discipline our bodies as well. If we only ever give in to our cravings, lethargy, or emotions, we won't accomplish much. Disciplining the body and exercising self-control is a way to honor God with your body. And if you still aren't convinced, Proverbs 31:17 says, "She sets about her work vigorously; her arms are strong for her tasks." If you ask me, I think that verse paints a beautiful picture of a woman who can handle a little physical labor. And in my mind, I like to think of her arms as not only strong but toned just the way we women like them.

Restoring the Soul

The truth is, we should be physically active because when we are, we increase our strength, mobility, and flexibility. We reduce stress. We have more energy. We sleep better, and oh yes, it can even help us lose weight. But it doesn't stop there. Hebrews 10:5 says, "Therefore, when Christ came into the world, he said: 'Sacrifice and offering you did not desire, but a body you prepared for me.'"

Think about it. Why did God give Jesus a human body? He did it for a couple reasons. In the human body, Jesus experienced the desires and passions of the flesh. Jesus understood what it felt like to live in a human body, and even though He remained sinless, He understood what it felt like to be tired, hungry, and maybe even crave a fig or two. (Okay, I don't know if He actually craved a fig, but you get my point.) I also don't know if Jesus ever struggled with His weight or felt out of shape. But He sure understood what it felt like to be mocked, abandoned, and beaten to a pulp. That said, Jesus modeled how to live life in the physical body following the will of God, and through His example, He demonstrated it is possible for us to do the same. God cares about your spiritual health, yes. But He also cares about your body and what you do with it because He cares about your overall well-being. "Beloved, I pray that all may go well with you and that you may be in good health, as it goes well with your soul" (3 John 1:2 ESV).

I think when it comes to our faith, we can fall into the trap of thinking of ourselves in two dimensions: physical and spiritual. There's my body, and then there's my soul. But the sum of who we are is everything without separation. We aren't just souls dropped into human bodies to live on earth until we die. Who we are is the entirety of our body, mind, soul, and spirit intermingled. When we take care of our physical body through exercise, what we get out of it is more than just the peripheral stuff we see.

> *Who we are is the entirety of our body, mind, soul, and spirit intermingled.*

Let the Truth Sink In

And whatever you do, whether in word or deed, do it all in the name of the Lord Jesus, giving thanks to God the Father through him.

—Col. 3:17

And the God of all grace, who called you to his eternal glory in Christ, after you have suffered a little while, will himself restore you and make you strong, firm and steadfast.

—1 Pet. 5:10

A lazy person does not roast his game, but a diligent person prizes his possessions.

—Prov. 12:27 TLV

Did you catch that last one? But the diligent person prizes their possessions. In other words, make good use of what God has given you and treasure it. Good stewardship of our body matters to God. Spending time exercising and taking care of your body is not a waste of time or energy. It's an investment in yourself so you can live more fully for the Lord.

The Double-Edged Sword

Just as a lack of exercise can be detrimental to the body, too much exercise can also be harmful. If you're like me and enjoy being physically active, there can be significant pitfalls when you exercise to the point of exhaustion or for reasons that become more about vanity and self-worth. I'm a prime example. I enjoy setting physical goals to achieve. Whether it's training for a marathon or taking part in a 30-day cycling challenge, I find great joy in the training and discipline when working toward a physical accomplishment. However, if you let the pursuit of the goal take over your life, it can lead to a false sense of self-worth and even false worship.

Before I knew who I was in Christ, I identified with my career, my accomplishments, and a perspective of who others thought I was. It wasn't until I no longer had the physical capability to move my body that I learned who I really was. I'm not saying I know without a doubt why I developed all my health issues. But I have a pretty good guess. It's because I had misaligned priorities and focused too much on the things I wanted and did not use my body to glorify God. When I look back at my own situation, I can see now that during the toughest season of my life, I was looking for a sense of accomplishment, maybe even a way to deal with the emotional pain I was experiencing. But God had bigger plans for me. Not only did He want me to know who I was, but He also wanted me to look to Him for dependence and direction, not try to find it on my own.

My friend, if you're an athlete or someone who finds great pleasure in being active, be sure to evaluate your motives and reasons for training as hard as you do. Does it glorify God? Do you push through pain in training just because of your ego? Is exercising more about being thin and looking good than anything else?

Whether you avoid exercise altogether or push yourself beyond healthy limits, neither approach honors God with your body. True balance is found when you fix your eyes on Him and follow His ways rather than your own. If you wrestle with inactivity, overexertion or self-worship, ask the Lord to help you find a healthy rhythm.

Let's pray.

Dear Heavenly Father,

I worship You for the thought and detail You put into creating me. Please forgive me if I haven't appreciated what You've created. Please help me care for my body by being active in a way that supports my well-being. I lift my struggles to You in complete faith, knowing with all my heart that Your strength will encourage and sustain me. Help me with motivation or provide me with a way to see exercise as an act of worship. I praise You for the good work You have prepared for my life, and I thank You. In Jesus's name, amen.

Restoring the Body

Objections to Overcome

We know by now that regular movement is good for our overall well-being. But even when the benefits are clear, it often takes more than logic to actually get started. Over the years, I've heard of many reasons why people avoid physical activity, and honestly, I get it. Life gets busy, motivation runs low, and sometimes the idea of working out just feels overwhelming. Here are a few common ones I've heard (and maybe even said myself).

- No time
- No money
- Don't like it
- Don't enjoy feeling hot or sweating
- It's painful
- Feel self-conscious
- Feel uncoordinated or weak
- Don't know what to do
- Fear of new or repeat injury

I don't want to minimize these reasons because to some degree, they're all understandable. But at some point, you have to draw a line in the sand and decide that you want something different. I can't make you want to exercise. Only you can make that choice. But what I can do is help you see that the things holding you back aren't as impossible to overcome as they might feel right now.

If you struggle with starting an exercise habit, realize that the first battle you need to overcome is the one in your mind. Often our heads hold us hostage before we've even laced up our shoes. Emotions have a way of highjacking our best intentions. If you struggle with the not-feeling-like-exercising-today mentality, don't give your mind a say in the matter. Decide you are going to do it and stick to the plan no matter what. Those feelings will disappear after you've completed your workout, and you'll be glad you kept your promise to yourself.

> *Often our heads hold us hostage before we've even laced up our shoes.*

Being active starts with the mind and requires literally taking the first step. It involves opening yourself up to new possibilities and becoming vulnerable. People have come to really dislike the saying "no pain, no gain," but sometimes it is true. Hebrews 12:11 (NLT) says, "No discipline is enjoyable while it is happening—it's painful! But afterward there will be a peaceful harvest of right living for those who are trained in this way."

Starting a new exercise habit can be painful. Your muscles will be sore in the beginning. Don't fear it. Now that you know pain is coming, you can prepare for it. (Buy some Epsom salts; pour 2 cups in a bathtub and have a warm soak after your workout. It helps relieve muscle soreness.)

Change requires effort, and that can be painful. But with God, all things are possible. Remember that athletes who want to win need to be intentional and disciplined. You want to win at building healthy lifestyle habits. Being intentional about becoming an active person and being disciplined will move you from where you are starting to where you want to end up.

Overcoming Fear and Embracing Vulnerability

Sometimes our hesitancy to exercise isn't that we don't genuinely want to work out. It's that we injured ourselves previously, and we're afraid of the injury or pain coming back. This is a real thing, I know. I once broke my toe in taekwondo, and it took me months to get back to the studio. Two things took up space in my mind before I finally got the courage to return to class. The first was that I was afraid if I kicked, I would break my toe again. The second was that I procrastinated returning to class, and the longer I was absent, the more afraid I became of what others would think of me for taking so long to return.

If you are dealing with the fear of pain or injury, I suggest getting a trusted coach, an expert in the field who can help you take the appropriate steps to injury recovery. Knowing you've got a coach you can trust to help can be the difference between staying down on the ground and getting back up again.

Second, we get so wrapped up in what other people think that it hinders the real progress we can make in our lives. We tend to make things worse by worrying about what other people think. We worry that they think we're too fat for the gym or too inflexible for yoga class. We worry about the back fat in our bathing suits or the sweaty armpits when we lift our arms. Do you know what I look like after a long run? My face is beet-red, and there's sweat salt all over my face and body. Flyaway hairs are around my forehead, and I don't smell great. But you know what people say when I'm out running? They don't say I look like a hot mess. They say, "Good for you; keep going!" (I'll talk more about how to deal with being self-conscious in Chapter 12: Be Beautiful).

Don't let fear or shame hold you back. Ask for help, and know that I'm here cheering you on. You've got this!

So whether you are a beginner just getting started with exercise or it's time for you to change up your workout routine, here are a few tips to help you get started.

- **Research an activity and decide what you need to execute it.** Do you need any specific equipment, a membership, or clothes for your chosen activity? Do you need to hire a trainer or coach? If yes, get what you need to start as soon as possible. Hint: If this process takes too long, costs more than you can afford, or seems too arduous, choose something else.

- **Make a plan and be specific.** For example, I will go to a 60-minute spin class at the studio beside my office three times per week after work.
- **Create a routine for consistency.** Business Coach Marie Forleo says, "If it ain't scheduled, it ain't real." Block off the time on your calendar and keep it as a standing appointment. Don't schedule other things during that time. It's your time. Usually, the same time each day works best. I like the morning so I get it out of the way, but you do you.
- **Start slowly, but be consistent.** Don't plan to run a marathon in four weeks if you can't even run around the block. Instead, walk or run 3–5 times a week over a few months, and you've created a consistent running habit with a marathon goal in sight.
- **Do something you're physically able to do.** Don't plan to learn how to surf if you don't live near the ocean and can't swim. Maybe start by taking swimming lessons and progress from there.
- **Be content with just getting it done, especially if you're a beginner or recovering from an injury.** Don't worry if it feels a bit awkward; that's perfectly normal. Your body is getting used to doing something new, so just give it time.
- **Do the same type of exercise for at least 4–12 weeks so you can track your progress.** That means doing the same fitness or dance class, strength training plan, running program, cycling routine, walking schedule, and so on. That doesn't mean you can't do anything else, like stretching after your workout. You just want to give yourself time to see if you like the activity you've chosen and assess how it's working for you.

Here's some motivation for when you don't feel like exercising.
- Put on some upbeat music to get you in the mood before you do anything.
- Get a new workout outfit, shoes, and water bottle that you'll look forward to using, and lay them out in plain sight. Do it the night before if you're an early morning riser.
- Get a new fitness tracker or app.
- Work out with a friend or group.
- Get support from people who will encourage you to get fit.
- Pray. Need I say more?

Here are some suggestions for the already active person who gets bored with their workouts.
- **Mix it up.** Do something different. For example, if you weight-train three times a week, try hiking or Pilates instead. Another option is to add it to your existing exercise program.
- **Learn how to do something new.** Learning a new skill not only cross-trains your body but also your mind. When I lived in Germany, I took ballroom dancing lessons. I was never an expert, but it was great exercise and a lot of fun. Sometimes, learning a new skill also involves researching it by watching videos, reading a book, or talking to experts.
- **Become the teacher.** If you have a passion for a specific sport or activity, why not teach it? I bet there are many people who admire something that comes easily to you. One way to regain passion for a skill is to teach it. It helps you become better at it and helps others in the process.
- **Thirty-day challenges and charity-based programs.** A great way to get motivated and train consistently is to take part in a 30-day challenge or sign up for a fundraising event. The possibilities are endless: 30-day yoga challenges, a charity

golf tournament, a bikeathon, or a 5K run. Sometimes all we need to get started is a little inspiration found when what we do helps others as well.
- **Join a club or a league, or work out with a friend.** We don't always have motivation on our own. Sometimes being around other like-minded individuals is a great way to stay accountable to your exercise program and meet new people. My mom wasn't too keen to exercise on her own. But when I agreed to take her to aqua-fit once a week, she started looking forward to going to class, and it was a great way for us to spend some time together.

When You Have No Time to Work Out

I'm not going to spend a lot of time on this because we talked a lot about time management in the previous chapters. But sometimes we really do have hectic schedules and get bogged down because we can't get to the gym or do the workout we had in mind. Here's another scenario that requires a mindset shift. Stop thinking about your workout in terms of a 60-minute class and start weaving more physical activity into your everyday schedule. Could you walk or cycle to work? On your next walk, could you add 10 lunges every 50 feet? Is it laundry day? Can you do a set of squats before and after you load the machine? While waiting for the kettle to boil, you could do a plank. After you brush your teeth, do some push-ups. Sometimes the issue isn't lack of time—it's simply learning to spot the opportunities we already have.

When Spending Money on Exercising Leaves a Bad Taste in Your Mouth

Maybe you've been there. You bought the gym membership or monthly pass and barely used it. You hired a trainer, but it got too expensive. You invested in that fancy piece of equipment, and now it's collecting dust in the corner. Believe it or not, you don't have to spend another dollar to start building an exercise habit. We often overthink what we need to begin, but the truth is that we just need to start. There are tons of free workout videos online. Many gyms offer free guest passes if you want to try it before committing. But if you're serious about moving your body, you can literally start right now.

> *We often overthink what we need to begin, but the truth is that we just need to start.*

Try this:
- 20 jumping jacks, 15 squats, 10 sit-ups, 5 push-ups
- Repeat 3–5 times, rest when needed, and drink your water

No cost. No catch. Just a little sweat and a step toward something better.

A Note to Those with Physical Limitations or Injuries

I haven't forgotten about you. You may face challenges that others don't, and I want you to know that your ability to honor God isn't limited by what your body can or can't do. Sometimes God uses our limitations to reveal His strength in powerful ways. If you have a limb you can move, move it. Do what you can with what you've been given. (Bethany Hamilton, a pro surfer, is a powerful example of this when she continued riding waves after losing her arm in a shark attack at age 13.)

And if you're in a season where movement isn't possible, that doesn't mean you're falling short. You can still care for your body, honor it, and honor God in the process. He sees you. He loves you. And He will use your life and your story for His glory.

Age is no excuse. When I owned my boot camp, I taught a co-ed class specifically for older adults, and let me tell you, they were some of the most inspiring people I've ever worked with. I affectionately called them the 60+ Ratpack (a little nod to Frank Sinatra, Dean Martin, and Sammy Davis Jr.). Most of them were in their late 60s to mid-70s, and yes, they did the same drills I gave my younger campers. They weaved through pylons, did side squats and shoulder presses, each at their own pace with their own limitations. Whether it was arthritis, a tricky knee, or limited shoulder mobility, they didn't let it stop them. We modified the exercises, they did what they could, and they gave it their best.

That class reminded me that fitness isn't about being the fittest; it's about showing up for the life you want. And mindset matters just as much as movement.

Conclusion

Last but not least, what exercises are best for weight loss? Friend, I wish it were as simple as telling you which magic exercise will do the trick. But it's not that simple. There is no one exercise that will melt away all the unwanted pounds because your physical activity is just part of the bigger equation—as you learned going through The Unhealthy Body Cycle: Part One and Part Two. The best advice I can offer for the beginner is this: The best exercise is the one you will consistently do.

As you become more fit, you will be able to assess the level of intensity that's right for you. Look for ways that challenge you. Don't do the same thing year after year. Your body will adapt to that level of intensity, distance, and weight, making it hard to see progress. Your body must be challenged to keep muscles balanced. Switch up your exercises every few weeks or months, change your intensity level, or learn a new skill within a sport. Not only will this keep your body and mind agile, but it will keep you from getting bored as well. "So whether you eat or drink, or whatever you do, do it all for the glory of God" (1 Cor. 10:31 NLT).

Review and Key Insights to Remember

- The sum of who you are includes your body, mind, soul, and spirit. Being active contributes to your overall well-being, and God wants you to be well.
- Disciplining the body through exercise helps you accomplish everyday tasks. It increases your strength, mobility, flexibility, and energy levels. It reduces stress, can assist with weight loss, and helps you sleep better.
- Keeping fit should never be about vanity first. View exercise as an act of worship.
- Becoming active starts with a decision and a mindset shift, and literally requires taking the first step. Just start.
- Feelings and motivation only get you so far. Be intentional about cultivating an active lifestyle. Have a plan, be consistent, and be disciplined. Hire a coach if you need help.

Your Surprise Package Has Arrived!

There's nothing like rewarding yourself with a delicious protein smoothie after a great workout. What I love about this one is the versatility. You can mix and match different types of berries, leafy greens, and flavored protein powder to give your taste buds something new to look forward to. Here's the base and a few of my favorite additions.

Very Berry Protein Smoothie

    Prep Time: 5 minutes
    Servings: 1–2

Ingredients:
    1 cup frozen blueberries
    ½ cup frozen strawberries
    ¾ cup frozen kale
    1½ cups unsweetened almond milk
    ½ cup cold water (coconut water is great too)
    1 large scoop vanilla protein powder, plant-based (as directed by brand)
    1 small scoop glutamine powder (as directed by brand)
    3 heaping tbsp. ground flaxseed (fiber)
    Optional: dash of cinnamon to taste

Note: if you prefer to use fresh instead of frozen, the quantity may vary. You also may want to add ice cubes.

Directions:
Place all ingredients in a high-speed blender. Blend 45–60 seconds until smooth. Pour into a tall glass and sprinkle with cinnamon. Enjoy!

Why add ground flaxseed or glutamine? Ground flaxseed is loaded with nutrients and rich in omega-3 fatty acids (good fats), which can help reduce cholesterol and lower blood pressure. It also adds some fiber to your smoothie, which will help you feel full longer and aid in digestion.

If you're a fitness enthusiast, you've probably heard of adding glutamine to your protein smoothie. It helps make proteins for muscle tissue. I add glutamine because it's also beneficial for the gut. Glutamine helps support the immune system as the amino acids help maintain your intestinal lining.

Chapter 10

Be Mindful: It Ain't No Careless Whisper

Sometimes I get so mad at myself—well, maybe *frustrated* is a better word for it. I can't tell you how many times I have been on my way to somewhere familiar when suddenly my mind wanders off the road and deep into my thoughts. While my eyes are still open and my hands are on the wheel, I see the traffic, acknowledge when to stop and go, and signal my turns. All seems to go smoothly, and I'm being a courteous driver. Deep into my thoughts, I replay a scenario in my mind or think about what I will do about this or that when suddenly—nooo! I miss my exit. Sheer panic propels me from my thoughts to the sudden dilemma. "Great, now I'm going to be late," I say. Immediately, I'm in panic mode, and because of my faux pas, I'm stuck in traffic. It's going to be another few miles before I can exit, and today of all days I left my house late. "How could this happen to me? Haven't I driven this same route a million times?" And yes, at this point, I'm angry at the fact that I just wasn't paying attention. I wish I had been more mindful of where I was going rather than so consumed with what I was thinking.

Our minds have a funny way of taking us out of a present situation and putting us in a place that's somewhere else in the past or the future. I think that's why the term "be present" has become such a common expression. People are realizing that it's easy to be physically present but in our minds be completely absent.

Being present is easier said than done, right? When it comes to our thoughts, we run into the danger of thinking too much. I think this rings especially true for women, and I wonder sometimes if we complicate things by overthinking ourselves.

I've heard women repeatedly complain about the burden of having to remember it all. It's why we have all the to-do lists, right? But who can keep track? Give the teacher a thank-you gift at the end of the school year. Remember to bring wine to the party for the hosts. Make the cupcakes for the bake sale at school. Send your nephew a birthday card and call your mom because it's been a while. Do you want to know what the worst part is? Who do you think gets blamed when your brother forgets to send you a birthday card? That's right—your sister-in-law. Because if he forgets, he's just a guy. But heaven forbid if she forgets. With all the constant list-making and reminders to help us navigate through the busyness of life, you'd think at some point we'd find our minds at ease and feel some sense of calm. Unfortunately, we often feel the exact opposite—frazzled and unable to just stop thinking.

I believe there is someone who thrives on keeping our minds so preoccupied that we miss the exit, forget something on the list, and get totally stressed out because of it. And I believe you know who it is—our enemy, Satan. That's right. He just loves to keep us so busy that we go through life, often with a mind so full that there's no room left for us to find any peace. He thrives on having us believe we have to do more, be more, and get more. And he places these thoughts in our minds when we're most vulnerable—during times of stress.

The problem is that when Satan floods our minds with lies or a million racing thoughts, he's trying to keep us distracted from God. And he's so cunning we often don't even realize who's behind all the chaos. He uses our thoughts to place doubt, inadequacy, and fear in our minds on a subconscious level. Once those thoughts are there, we think about them. And the more we try not to think about them, the more we do. Well, guess what. There's actually a scientific explanation for why this happens. As neuroscientist Dr. Caroline Leaf says, "A thought is a real physical thing that occupies mental real estate in the brain and mind." She also says, "Whatever we think about the most will grow" (Leaf 2021, 133,137). That's the neuroscience of the brain. So how you think repeatedly becomes your go-to thinking pattern. Think about those doubts, fears, and insecurities long enough, and you start to believe them.

Understanding the Complexity of the Mind

It's easy to assume when we talk about the mind that we're talking about the brain. But the brain is only the physical part of the body that is controlled by the mind. The mind is divided into three parts. Most of our mind activity is in our nonconscious mind. The nonconscious mind is the part we're not really paying attention to, but it runs 24/7. It holds our deep beliefs and attitudes. It's where our memories are stored and is in constant conversation with our conscious and subconscious mind. The conscious mind is our fully aware state. It's where we actively know what we're thinking, saying, and doing. And the subconscious mind is the part in the middle. It's the level where we are slightly aware of our thoughts and where they move from the conscious to the nonconscious mind (Leaf 2021, 146).

So why is this important? Changing the way you think is the key to changing your actions. When the same actions are repeated on a consistent basis, you begin to form habits. That applies to us on a physical level and a thought level as well. If you want to cultivate new health habits, you need to make a conscious effort with your head before any actions follow. The problem is that if you don't believe you

> *If you want to cultivate new health habits, you need to make a conscious effort with your head before any actions follow.*

can change, you won't because a new action requires a new thought pattern. That's why changing the way you think is the first step in learning how to build healthy habits that will last.

Be Mindful is about how our thoughts have the power to influence our actions. And if we learn how to transform our thoughts, we can transform the way we think, speak, behave, and ultimately live our lives.

Romans 12:2 says, "Do not conform to the pattern of this world, but be transformed by the renewing of your mind. Then you will be able to test and approve what God's will is—his good, pleasing and perfect will." That means that through the power of the Holy Spirit, we can transform our minds and lives when we walk in obedience to the truth found in God's Word.

So, what do we do?

First, we must be aware that though Satan can influence our thoughts, he has no power over us unless we give it to him. We must recognize that he's out to destroy us in any way he can, and he's trying to access our minds to do it. He even influences the lies we tell ourselves. And we do it all the time. We think, "Oh, it's not that bad" or that we're fine even though we're not. We frequently act on our impulses, fail to notice important details, and even jump to wrong conclusions. We all have blind spots and can't always tell ourselves the truth because we don't stop to really think about what the truth is. Instead, we just keep going, forever running behind and being overwhelmed by the expectations society places on us. We start believing the lies. And if Satan can get us to believe the lies, we're walking in the danger zone to sin.

The Bible says, "For though we live in the world, we do not wage war as the world does. The weapons we fight with are not the weapons of the world. On the contrary, they have divine power to demolish strongholds" (2 Cor. 10:3-4).

Paul, who wrote Corinthians, says that our job in this battle is to destroy strongholds. A stronghold can be a mental block or anything with a hold on your thought patterns. It can also be a personal attitude, a worry, or being consumed with seeking the approval of others. It can be pride, lust, pleasure, and greed. It can be anything you make into an idol in your life such as guilt, fear, resentment, or insecurity. In his book *When the Enemy Strikes*, Charles F. Stanley writes, "Habitual patterns of thinking become strongholds in our minds" (Stanley 2004, 77). The Apostle Paul used the term *stronghold* to describe a mindset or attitude, and he tells us we are to tear them down (2 Cor. 10:3-6).

Destructive Thoughts Create a Toxic Mind

A tragic story in the Bible reveals what can happen when we entertain a thought we just can't get out of our mind.

> *One evening David got up from his bed and walked around on the roof of the palace. From the roof he saw a woman bathing. The woman was very beautiful, and David sent someone to find out about her. The man said, "She is Bathsheba, the daughter of Eliam and the wife of Uriah the Hittite." Then David sent messages to get her. She came to him, and he slept with her. (Now she was purifying herself from her monthly uncleanliness.) Then she went back home.*
> —2 Sam. 11:2-4

The Bible doesn't say what the timeline was from when King David saw Bathsheba to when he had her summoned, but we can only assume that when he saw Bathsheba bathing, the thought of sleeping with her became a stronghold—a repeated thought pattern that played over and over in his mind until he acted on it. We might call this temptation that led to sin. And though not all thoughts are temptations that lead to sin, with Be Mindful, we must understand the power our thoughts have over our behavior. Just as our body can become toxic through poor digestion and overburdened organs, our minds can become toxic if we don't take the time to examine our thoughts.

From a health perspective, this is where we women fall into the trap of failure before we have even made any changes to our lifestyle. You've likely tried many diets or exercise programs in the past, but somewhere along the line, you fell back into old habits that made it hard for you to stick to your new routine. But you really need to consider something here. When you fell back into those old habits, it was likely because of the thoughts you entertained repeatedly before you even started—thoughts like "I've never been able to keep the weight off. I've never been able to control my cravings. I've always had a slow metabolism." These thoughts, or shall we just call them lies, have become strongholds in your life. The good news is that we can learn how to tear down these strongholds step by step when we begin to discern our thoughts, focus on truth, interrupt our thought patterns, and guard our minds.

Restoring the Soul
Discern Your Thoughts

> *We demolish arguments and every pretension that sets itself up against the knowledge of God, and we take captive every thought to make it obedient to Christ.*
>
> —2 Cor. 10:5

Learning how to discern our thoughts is a crucial step in changing the way we think. We tend to feel that if we think something, it must be true because it comes from within us. But just because you think something doesn't make it true. Training the mind to stop, consciously reflect, and discern our thoughts helps us understand what kind of thoughts they are and how they may subconsciously influence our behavior. You can ask yourself, "Where is this thought coming from? God? Satan? Or is it just random?"

> *Beloved, do not believe every spirit, but test the spirits to see whether they are from God, for many false prophets have gone out into the world.*
> —1 John 4:1 ESV

One way to know where a thought is coming from is to ask yourself, "Is this a destructive thought? Is it congruent with what the Bible says about me?" Asking yourself these questions can help you recognize when thoughts are affecting the way you feel about yourself. Ephesians 6:10–18 (as you read in Chapter 8: Be Healthy, Part Three) helps us understand that through the power of the Holy Spirit living within us as Christians, we have the power to cast out destructive and debilitating thoughts by using God's Word, the sword of the Spirit.

So if your thought is something like "I'll never be able to overcome my battle with food," you can cast it out by saying, "I cast out this thought of never being able to overcome my battle with food, in Jesus's name."

By stopping to discern your thoughts, you are training your mind to take subconscious thoughts and bring them to your conscious mind. This takes practice, but it can be done. If you've ever taken part in mindful meditation, it's a bit like that. You stop to notice a thought. The difference is that you take it a step further by using the power of the Holy Spirit to help you transform your thinking patterns.

If you notice thoughts that persistently rob you of peace—thoughts laced with doubt, fear, anger, jealousy, comparison, and so on—it's a clue that you're not just dealing with something random. Don't underestimate the power of our enemy. He's not some cute little guy in a red pajama onesie with a pitchfork. He's real, and he's a true enemy, always fighting against us. He wants to destroy you in any way he can. He'll use your insecurities, bad habits, relationships, addictions, and anything and everything in between to sabotage your healthy efforts. Don't be afraid. You have Jesus on your side, and you know Who has already won.

Focus on Truth

Just before Jesus started His ministry, the Holy Spirit led Him into the desert to be tempted by the devil. And what did Satan do? He waited until Jesus had fasted for 40 days and 40 nights and was hungry when he tempted Him with the idea of food. "The tempter came to Him and said, 'If you are the Son of God, tell these stones to become bread.' Jesus answered, 'It is written: "Man shall not live on bread alone, but on every word that comes from the mouth of God"'" (Matt. 4:3–4).

Notice what Jesus did. He used Scripture to fight back. The next time you deal with the thought of "I'll never be able to change," take it a step further and say, "I cast out this thought of never being able to change my ways in Jesus's name because the Bible says, 'Therefore, if anyone is in Christ, he is a new creation. The old has passed away; behold, the new has come'" (2 Cor. 5:17 ESV). Say that scripture out loud. Scripture is God's breathed Word, and because it's of God, its authority is powerful.

Destructive thought patterns create toxic overload in our minds. Just like cancer cells replicate and take over healthy cells, destructive thought patterns do the same. They take over the real estate of our mind and create a toxic environment. We're not always quick to recognize those paralyzing thoughts. But if you notice those thoughts every time you're trying to instill a positive change, it's time to get out your sword and slay them.

Not all of Satan's attempts to derail us are that obvious though. Have you ever found yourself thinking about a situation you just can't get out of your mind? Maybe it was an argument you had with a friend, and you wished things had played out differently. Maybe there's an uncomfortable discussion you need to have with your supervisor, and you can't stop worrying about what will be said. Or maybe you've been treated unfairly and can't stop thinking about how hurt you are. These thoughts may not necessarily fall under the category of thoughts from God or thoughts from Satan. It's just life, right? But ask yourself this: How long am I going to keep thinking about this? An hour? Two? All day long? Ruminating or worrying over a situation without coming to a resolution is a sure way to keep you stuck and distracted from moving forward in life. Sometimes when I can't get my mind to stop thinking, it's the clue that I need to do something different.

Interrupt Your Thought Patterns

One of the hardest things about writing a book is setting aside the time to do it and then not being able to find the words. I've blocked aside precious time to write, and when I'm sitting there staring at a blank screen, every minute that passes becomes more and more frustrating. I start thinking, *"If I don't write something soon, I'll have wasted my time and accomplished nothing."*

Or I start writing and think, *"It's just not flowing the way it should. This is terrible."* The harder I try to write, the worse it gets. I think, *"I've tried to cast out negative thoughts, and they're not going away."* So I just sit there getting more and more upset.

Our thought-battles often take longer to win. If you find your mind on repeat and you can't seem to stop that broken record player no matter what, it's time to pull the cord out of the socket.

When my stress level soars and my mind can't stop racing, a plunge into a cold lake is all I need to change the tune. You'd be surprised how much you won't think about your problems when you're shivering and can barely catch your breath. Plunging into the lake has taught me to leave the worries under water and come up knowing Jesus is there with me.

Interrupt your thoughts by changing your physical space and doing something to distract you from your thoughts. Try going for a run or walking in nature. Take a cold shower or organize your closet. You get the point. Interrupting your thoughts can help you shift your state of mind. Once your mind has had a little break, focus on progress rather than problems.

Guard Your Mind

By now you've come to realize how important our thoughts are when it comes to our behavior. But being mindful isn't just about analyzing our thought patterns. It's also about discerning what we allow into our minds in the first place. We can do this consciously by making an effort to act on what values are important to us.

I'll give you an example. A few months ago, my husband and I were at an outdoor café sipping on cappuccinos. Quietly engaged in conversation, we enjoyed listening to the sound of a man playing his guitar and singing some tunes in the background. Suddenly, his words caught my attention, and I didn't like what I heard. The lyrics to his song were about how the devil had told him twice that he'd be standing at the Pearly Gates and that God would turn him away because he hadn't turned good enough in time to go to heaven. Admittedly, I was a little rattled listening to his song. *How could he inflict those lyrics on us poor, "innocent" patrons?* Just as I was about to get up and walk away, I heard the whisper that interrupted my thoughts. This man didn't need my judgment. He needed my compassion. Did he really believe the words he was singing? And finally, what had I read in my Bible just that morning?

I had read that Jesus's sacrifice of dying on the cross for our sins was not meant to be kept secret. Instead, it is meant to be shared as good news. If we don't know Christ, our sins separate us from having a relationship with God. The good news is that because Jesus took the punishment for our sins when He died on the cross, conquered death, and rose again, we don't need to do anything to earn salvation. If we truly believe in what Christ has done for us, we need to ask Him to forgive us our sins and ask Him to come live in our hearts so we never have to worry about being good enough again. And that's because we're not—Jesus is. And He's all we need to get through the Pearly Gates.

The man playing the guitar and singing his tunes needed to hear this. How awful it would be if he went through life with no one ever telling Him about Jesus. I hesitated and thought, *Seriously God, you really want me to get up and confront this guy in front of a crowd?* As I finally gathered up the courage to talk to him, he quickly began another song and then another and another. Finally, I finished my cappuccino and wrote him a note, which I placed in his tip box.

There are three things we can learn from this story: (1) It's important to guard the mind, so getting up and leaving might have been exactly what I needed to do to stop that song from playing over and over in my mind. (Isn't it just so annoying when you can't get a song out of your head?) (2) God can use moments like that to convict our hearts and show compassion to those who don't know Christ. You just have to be willing to pause and discern where the whisper is coming from. (3) I wish I had spoken to him rather than taken the easy way out and left a note. Please pray I'll have more courage to do it next time.

By training our minds to discern our thoughts and focus on God's truth, we become better equipped at guarding our minds. Give the Wellness Whisperer a chance to occupy some of that precious real estate in your mind. If you listen to Him, you just might change your tune.

> *Give the Wellness Whisperer a chance to occupy some of that precious real estate in your mind.*

Let the Truth Sink In

Colossians 3:1-3 reminds us, "Since, then, you have been raised with Christ, set your hearts on things above, where Christ is, seated at the right hand of God. Set your minds on things above, not on earthly things. For you died, and your life is now hidden with Christ in God."

Philippians 4:8 says, "Finally brothers and sisters, whatever is true, whatever is noble, whatever is right, whatever is pure, whatever is lovely, whatever is admirable—if anything is excellent or praiseworthy—think about such things."

Proverbs 15:14 (NLT) says, "A wise person is hungry for knowledge, while the fool feeds on trash."

Learning how to guard your mind is twofold. Line up your values with your follow-through actions and focus your mind on God's truth.

One way our mind is flooded with trash is through the use of social media. Don't get me wrong. There are some positive things we get from social media—connection, education, inspiration. But how many times have you found yourself looking at those feeds for much longer than you intended? How many times have you seen ads or videos that have no relevance for you, but those images and cuss words went into your mind, and now you can't stop thinking about them? You didn't want those thoughts in your mind, but somehow, there they are. If you're not guarding your mind, you're subjecting yourself to words and images that can create real thoughts in your head, whether or not you like them.

Discerning what you allow into your mind takes practice. Realize that thoughts can come from literally anywhere—things you read, things you watch, things you listen to, people you surround yourself with, and so on. Be on guard and evaluate what and who you'll allow to influence you.

Practical Wisdom

Don't let social media capture your attention first thing in the morning. If you want to reduce toxic overload in the mind, choose to avoid all forms of it until after you've spent some time with God. Ask Him to help you focus on seeking Him throughout the day. That will help guard your mind from distractions and keep the truth at the forefront.

Being mindful takes practice and is a lifelong pursuit to be more Christ-like. We may never have perfect thoughts. We may never always do what is right. But with the Holy Spirit, we can learn to train our minds and transform our behavior.

> *We may never have perfect thoughts. We may never always do what is right. But with the Holy Spirit, we can learn to train our minds and transform our behavior.*

Be mind-full of the Word of God. Be mind-less in believing debilitating thoughts. Don't give Satan the power to create toxic overload in your mind. And if you find yourself giving in to sin repeatedly, repent and ask the Heavenly Father to help you. Trust in the Lord that you can renew your mind. He will help you through His holy Word.

> *Those who live according to the flesh have their minds set on what the flesh desires; but those who live in accordance with the Spirit have their minds set on what the Spirit desires.*
> —Rom. 8:5

Let's pray.

Dear Heavenly Father,

Thank You for the mind-changing power found in Your Word. I know I don't always think the best thoughts or do what is right. Please forgive me when I have thought or said hurtful things to myself or others. Help me discern thoughts that are not beneficial for me, and help me make decisions based on Your Word. Instead of believing Satan's lies, remind me of Your infinite knowledge and immeasurable wisdom. I deeply desire to transform my mind with Your guidance to follow through with actions that align with my health goals. I praise You and thank You, knowing that Your power destroys every stronghold of the enemy in my life. In Jesus's name, amen.

Restoring the Body

It's time to remove some toxins. Just as toxic overload in the mind is detrimental to your mental and spiritual health, toxic overload in the body can be detrimental to your physical health. So let's start with how we can cleanse the body without getting totally freaked out about the word *cleanse*. Before you start cutting back on caffeine, sugar, alcohol, and deep-fried and processed food, it's important to note that the body naturally cleanses and detoxifies itself all on its own. It does this through enzymes in the body that continuously break down toxins and flush them out. We also have specific organs in the body—the skin, the liver, the colon, the kidneys, and the lungs—that assist in the process. We can optimize how the body releases these toxins when we consume fruits and vegetables that are packed with vital nutrients that boost the productivity of our enzymes (like my Roasted Beet and Pistachio Salad in Chapter 6). And while reducing or eliminating certain foods and beverages can be beneficial, I want to offer you some additional suggestions as well.

Here are five things you can do to assist in cleansing the body without going on a cleanse.

1. **Drink more filtered water.** It cleanses the body by removing waste. Herbal tea is good too.
2. **Add sulfur-containing foods** that help eliminate heavy metals such as mercury and cadmium. Some examples include broccoli, onions, and garlic, just to name a few.
3. **Switch to natural beauty and cleaning products** that don't contain harmful chemicals that mess with your hormones and wreak havoc on the body's ability to cleanse.
4. **Open your windows for fresh air** and add plants to your indoor space for better air quality. Breathe in that fresh air while doing your deep-breathing exercises (Chapter 6).
5. **Sweat.** Our skin is a wonderful tool God gave us to help us excrete toxins. Spend time in a sauna, steam room, or hot bath with Epsom salts.

Giving your cleansing organs a well-needed break is a great way to clean up your insides. The key to cleansing is to keep a healthy attitude about it. Contrary to popular practice, it isn't supposed to be a rapid weight loss tool. Its purpose is to assist your body in what it can already do on its own, with just a little help.

Finally, cleansing the body can be powerful for the mind as well. When we let the body release toxins, we benefit from the improved ability to better focus and draw our attention to what really matters most.

Conclusion

Be Mindful in assessing which thoughts and habits bring you closer to your healthy living goals. Commit to doing the daily work of thinking them through before you act. Transforming your thoughts will transform your actions, and when you learn how to shift debilitating thoughts to those with biblical truth, you'll experience how powerful the mind can be.

Review and Key Insights to Remember

- Be Mindful refers to how our thoughts have the power to influence our actions. If we learn how to transform our thoughts, we can transform our behavior.
- Habitual thought patterns can both help and harm you, depending on what you're thinking.
- You can change the way you think and tear down strongholds by discerning your thoughts, focusing on God's truth, interrupting your thought patterns, and guarding your mind.
- If you want to create healthy lifestyle habits, you must learn (and practice) how to transform your thoughts.
- The body naturally has the ability to cleanse itself. You can help it along by drinking more water and herbal tea, consuming nutrient-dense foods, and limiting exposure to harmful chemicals.

Your Surprise Package Has Arrived!

Your feet are the base of support and the foundation of movement. Each time you take a step, twice the weight of your body impacts the ground. But a lot of people don't like their feet, often as a result of foot problems or just simply because they don't think their feet look nice. Now just imagine if a disciple told Jesus not to wash his feet because he had uneven toes. I wonder if Jesus would have said, "You're right. I can handle dirty, smelly feet, but I draw the line with uneven toes." Let's change what we think about our feet by giving them the love and care they deserve with this simple-to-make, all-natural, toxin-free foot scrub.

Gimme Some Lov'n Foot Scrub

Ingredients:
- 1 cup sugar
- ½ cup extra virgin olive oil
- 3 tbsp. honey
- ½ tsp. lemon, freshly squeezed

Directions:
Pour ingredients into a small to medium-sized bowl and mix well. Then soak your feet in a large bowl of water or a tub. Optional: Add ½ cup Epsom salts. Rinse. Lather the scrub onto your feet, massaging it gently onto one foot, ankle, and calf and then onto the other. I recommend 2–10 minutes, longer if you like. Rinse and pat dry. Feel free to use this scrub on your entire body for soft, silky, radiant skin.

Chapter 11

Be Kind: Pay It Inward

I was in Florida, warmly bundled up on what Floridians might call a cold day with temperatures in the 50s. Gasp! As I stood in the gift shop browsing for a birthday card to send to a friend, a few words caught my attention as I read the inside: "I no longer call them hot flashes; I prefer to call them short, private tropical vacations." That's when it hit me. The very card I was holding in my hand reminded me of the same thing I was experiencing at that exact moment—an extreme fluctuation in temperature from one day to the next.

Back home in Ontario, Canada, I've actually come to experience this often, especially over the past 10 years. Our spring has almost disappeared. More often than not, it has stayed cold throughout May, and when June hits, so does summer. It goes from frigid single digits and wind chills to hot and humid almost overnight. And just when you think you know how to dress for the season, the temperature can change in an instant. Some might attribute this irregular weather pattern to the result of global warming or possibly the El Niño effect. Or is it La Niña? Either way, both are complex weather patterns resulting from variations in ocean temperatures in the equatorial

Pacific. While El Niño is the warm phase and La Niña is the cold phase, they both can influence the atmospheric weather around the globe and leave a lasting, devastating impact on our environment ("What Are El Niño and La Niña?" 2023).

Of course, all of this got me thinking about the human body. Our official body temperature may not fluctuate like the extreme fluctuations of the ocean, but sometimes our weight or diet habits can. And while these fluctuations may not warrant a global crisis, they sure can wreak havoc on the state of our physical, mental, and spiritual health, especially when we go from one dieting extreme to another, over and over again.

Be Kind refers to two things. First, we want to avoid all dieting extremes. Yo-yo dieting (aka weight cycling), binging, and starving wreak havoc on our bodies similar to the El Niño and La Niña effects. They are polar opposites and leave the body in a state of disaster, much like emotional eating. The results of repeatedly eating for reasons other than hunger often leave us feeling stuffed but never satisfied. Sadly, this way of eating and dieting is destroying our bodies, our minds, and our health.

Disclaimer: The intention of this chapter is to help you release the desire to diet in order to lose weight. My aim is to offer suggestions to help you build a better relationship with food, your body, and your faith. That said, I am not a trained expert in eating disorders. If you suffer from one or suspect you have one, please consult with a trained counselor or medical physician. If you struggle with any type of disordered eating, know this: You are not alone. Jesus is with you. He wants to help you break free of the pain you are feeling because you are so worthy, so valued, and so loved.

In researching for this chapter, it startled me to discover just how much of a problem dieting has become. Notice the following statistics.

- According to a study published in the *Journal of Psychopathology and Clinical Science*, thinking about dieting, a desire for thinness, fear of weight gain, feeling like you are overeating, and feelings of guilt predict eating disorder severity in those diagnosed with an eating disorder (Levinson et al. 2022). (I wonder how many people are suffering with these symptoms who haven't been officially diagnosed with an eating disorder.)
- In the United States, 69%–84% of women experience body dissatisfaction and prefer to have a smaller figure compared to the one they currently have (Runfola et al. 2013).
- According to a 10-year study done by the National Institutes of Health, dieting and disordered eating behaviors that started in adolescence were likely to continue well into young and middle adulthood (Neumark-Sztainer et al. 2011).
- A woman spends over 17 years of her life on a diet. The average woman diets twice per year ("The Average Woman Spends 17 Years of Her Life on Diets" 2012). This article is on the MedicalDaily website, and though I'm not sure how accurate the website is, these statistics seem highly probable, especially if women started dieting in their teens.
- The global weight loss and weight management diet market size was valued at $192.2 billion and is expected to reach $295.3 billion by 2027 (Vig and Deshmukh 2021).
- Of those who diet, most will regain their lost weight in one to five years ("Methods for Voluntary Weight Loss and Control: NIH Technology Assessment Conference Panel" 1992). Given this study was done in 1992, I wonder why people are still dieting in 2025.

- About 75% of women surveyed in a study by *SELF* magazine in partnership with the University of North Carolina at Chapel Hill have unhealthy thoughts, feelings, or behaviors related to food or their bodies ("Three Out of Four American Women Have Disordered Eating, Survey Suggests" 2008).
- About 39% of the above-surveyed women say concerns about what they eat or weigh interfere with their happiness ("Three Out of Four American Women Have Disordered Eating, Survey Suggests" 2008).

What's the Forecast?

The fact that dieting is a major problem in our society is obvious. But how do we stop this unhealthy way of living or avoid it in the first place? Perhaps a little lesson from the weather girl can point us in the right direction.

When meteorologists refer to stable conditions, it means the weather will not change quickly. Weather is strongly affected by how stable or unstable the atmosphere is. Stable air means the weather is likely to be calm or mild. Even if it's not great weather, it will not change abruptly. Unstable air can bring turbulence and severe weather ("Air Masses: Safety Spotlight: Air Masses and Fronts").

That's why when it comes to how we treat our body, we want to be kind to it by providing stable conditions. And we can find these stable conditions in Jesus who offers us the perfect stability we need to put a stop to harmful dieting behavior.

A Lesson in Sailing and How Jesus Calmed the Storm

Mark chapter 4 provides us insight into how Jesus offers us these stable conditions. But before I get to the scripture, I need to give you the back story. At the beginning of the chapter, Jesus is teaching in parables (short stories using familiar scenes to explain scriptural truth) to a large crowd of people. After teaching all day, Jesus's 12 disciples approach Him in private and ask Him to explain a parable in further detail. Jesus does so, and then He's tired. That is where we start our story.

> *That day when evening came, he said to his disciples, "Let us go over to the other side." Leaving the crowd behind, they took him along, just as he was, in the boat. There were also other boats with him. A furious squall came up, and the waves broke over the boat, so that it was nearly swamped. Jesus was in the stern, sleeping on a cushion. The disciples woke him and said to him, "Teacher, don't you care if we drown?" He got up, rebuked the wind and said to the waves, "Quiet! Be still!" Then the wind died down and it was completely calm. He said to his disciples, "Why are you so afraid? Do you still have no faith?" They were terrified and asked each other, "Who is this? Even the wind and the waves obey him!"*
>
> —Mark 4:35–41

When the disciples encountered the storm on the water, the text suggests they were genuinely afraid for their lives. It must have been some storm for experienced fishermen to panic to the extent that they had to wake Jesus up from His well-earned nap. The storm was terrifying. They were afraid they'd drown. They saw Jesus sleeping and thought He didn't care. But notice what Jesus did first. He told the wind and the sea to be still, and they were immediately calm. Then He rebuked His disciples for not having faith in Him. The story ended with them being in complete awe because of the power they witnessed that Jesus had over nature.

I think it's easy for us to look at these verses and criticize the disciples for their lack of faith. But isn't it interesting how Jesus had just spent all day teaching parables about hearing the Word of God and then, when the disciples were faced with a life-threatening storm (circumstance), they forgot the very lessons Jesus taught earlier that day? They were lessons that talked about not just hearing the Word but living it out through faith. I have to admit that I don't think I'd be better than any of Jesus's disciples. How often have I read the Bible, journaled my prayers, and then, when push came to shove, forgotten the exact thing I vowed to remember?

Perhaps I even take Jesus's presence with me for granted. As Christians, we know Jesus is always with us. He's in our hearts. He never leaves us or forsakes us. And the disciples, well, they had Jesus physically right there with them in the back of the boat. But is it possible that we put Jesus in the back of our minds until a storm comes along and we get angry with Him when we think He doesn't care about our problems? Maybe the lesson to be learned from the Bible is that instead of asking Jesus if He cares, we ought to ask Him if He will help.

I think it's safe to assume we've all lived through some bad weather in our lives, maybe even a few terrifying storms. When you experience a storm on the water, there are extreme winds and high waves. The boat rocks side to side and up and down. It can be a frightening and life-threatening situation. I think our daily routine can often turn out the same way. As we begin the day, things start out pretty calm. We go about our usual business and make healthy choices, and everything seems to be smooth sailing. Then suddenly something unexpected comes our way. Circumstances and emotions change quickly. There's frustration, disappointment, anger, anxiety, loneliness, boredom, depression, and possibly even shame or self-loathing. Yo-yo dieting with bouts of starving, binging, and emotional eating is often like sailing on smooth waters until, from seemingly out of nowhere, you end up in the middle of a storm. You frantically try to steer to safety and then realize you've lost command of the helm. Now you're out of control.

The Danger Zone of Extremes

How can we learn to identify extremes? These clues can help us.

- Do you frequently try the latest diet fad, swear it works, but then eventually put the weight back on?
- Do you eat all the junk food in the house on the weekend and then start a new diet on Monday?
- Do you eat healthy all day and binge at night?
- Do you eat healthy all week and gorge on the weekends?
- Do you weigh yourself daily and restrict food or exercise excessively if you've gained a couple of pounds?
- Does exercise entitle you to indulge in gluttonous eating?
- Do you feel like there's anything you're addicted to or can't live without?
- Does counting calories and tracking food intake on an app interfere with your relationship with food or your self-image?

Did You Know?

There is an eating disorder called orthorexia nervosa. People with orthorexia can become obsessively fixated on healthy eating and therefore adopt an extremely restrictive diet, often cutting out several food groups. It has less to do with weight loss or counting calories and more to do with the purity or cleanliness of their food. Though this eating disorder is not that common, it is an extreme behavior and something to be on the lookout for ("Orthorexia" 2024).

I know it's hard to acknowledge that these eating patterns and behaviors could be more of a problem than you care to admit, but I think taking an honest look at them is a crucial step in overcoming food and diet frustration. When we're riding the waves of extremes, it's often because we forget to give Jesus control of our circumstances. But have you noticed the more we try to control, the less we actually succeed? That's because God never meant for us to depend on ourselves.

Restoring the Soul

Though we may experience storms in life and unexpected, difficult situations, we must hold onto Jesus as our anchor, the One who provides us with those stable conditions through faith and trust in Him. Emotional eating shows up when we are looking to fill a need. Satan plants this deception so craftly because he knows our vulnerabilities. He often uses food to disguise his evil ways, making us believe we must go on a diet to lose weight, starve ourselves to be thin, or binge on whatever we're craving. Then he turns around and accuses us of guilt for our lack of discipline or willpower.

How does yo-yo dieting and emotional eating leave us feeling? It paints the illusion that we can take charge of a situation but quickly leaves us feeling helpless and out of control. And think about the term *yo-yo dieting*. It's no coincidence that as you diet, the yo-yo descends, and it feels great to be rid of the weight. But beware that once that diet is over, that yo-yo springs up faster than you can handle it, and then the cycle begins all over again.

When we are making unconscious choices regarding our eating habits, we don't realize that our true cravings may not be for food at all. We must learn how to pause, observe the circumstance around us, and not get swept away by the choppy waves of emotions. We must acknowledge that food or dieting is not our solution. Faith is. And when we ask God for help, we can trust He will give it to us. "So do not fear, for I am with you; do not be dismayed, for I am your God. I will strengthen you and help you; I will uphold you with my righteous right hand" (Isa. 41:10).

How can we Be Kind to ourselves? First, we can anchor ourselves to Jesus and allow Him to steer us to safety. We need to trust that He knows our destination and He's perfectly capable of calming the storms just as He did for the disciples. We may not always be able to avoid a storm, but what's important is acknowledging that He's with us during them. When we look to Jesus instead of food to fulfill our emotional and spiritual needs, He provides us with the stability we need to navigate through life. That helps us learn to find a balance between eating food for nourishment and enjoyment without the constant extremes like yo-yo dieting.

What Does Balanced Eating Look Like?

Balanced eating is learning to identify what makes up healthy eating in order to sustain a lifelong healthy relationship with food, your body, your mind, and your spirit. Balanced eating isn't about having to choose between foods that are good for you and foods that are bad for you. It's about helping you make wise, conscious decisions that line up with your health and life goals.

Tips for Balanced Eating

Avoid dieting. Restriction and deprivation create more weight problems in the long run because they sabotage your relationship with food and your body. We want to eat for nourishment and enjoyment, without guilt or condemnation. Instead of asking, "What do I need to cut out?" try asking, "What can I add to support my body today?" Go back to your food log in Chapter 8 and assess the following:

> *Restriction and deprivation create more weight problems in the long run because they sabotage your relationship with food and your body.*

- Are there any foods you can swap for healthier versions? Try replacing white or whole wheat bread with sprouted grain options such as Ezekiel bread or using coconut wraps that are gentler on digestion and kinder to your gut lining.
- Can you cut the portion size of a comfort food in half and add a big salad or steamed veggies? Pairing nourishing foods with the meals you already love is a gentle way to retrain your

taste buds and shift your habits without feeling deprived. Food is meant to be a blessing, not a battle.
- Can you give yourself permission to enjoy the occasional dessert, favorite meal, or night out without guilt? Remember, the goal isn't perfection; it's peace. The more you care for your body without punishment or pressure, the easier it becomes to make choices rooted in love, not fear. Balanced eating isn't about sticking to rules. It's about learning to trust yourself again.

Anchor Yourself to Truth and Feed on God's Word

Why spend money on what is not bread, and your labor on what does not satisfy? Listen, listen to me, and eat what is good, and you will delight in the richest of fare.
—Isa. 55:2

Forget moderation. Ditch the popular belief to eat everything in moderation. Sometimes eating everything doesn't agree with you, and sometimes our idea of moderation is a lot more than it should be. Become your own food detective. Pay attention to which foods give you energy, digest well, and help you feel your best. Discern which foods make you feel tired, bloated, moody, or gassy. This takes time, but it is worthwhile in helping you make your own healthy eating choices. And just a note here: Not all foods deemed as healthy will feel good for you, so don't feel the pressure to eat them if they don't.

Anchor Yourself to Truth and Feed on God's Word

So whether you eat or drink or whatever you do, do it all for the glory of God.
—1 Cor. 10:31

Learn to identify hunger cues. Are you truly hungry, or are emotions driving you to eat? Eat when you are hungry, but be mindful of your portion sizes. Just because you are hungry doesn't mean you should eat everything in sight. Slow down, take a few deep breaths, and bring attention to the present moment. Learn to identify when you begin to feel full, not bursting at the seams. Ask yourself, "Have I had enough?" Sometimes we eat more than we should just because it's on our plate. Beware of the following thoughts: "There's not enough for leftovers, so I'll just eat the rest" or "There are starving people in the world; I can't throw this out" or "This is so good I just can't help myself." If these thoughts are controlling your portion sizes, use a smaller plate. Or dish out what you'd normally eat and put half of it in a container for tomorrow. If you are still genuinely hungry, you can always go back and get some more.

Anchor Yourself to Truth and Feed on God's Word

If you find honey, eat just enough—too much of it, and you will vomit.

—Prov. 25:16

Cultivate awareness of your triggers, emotions, and behavior. Keeping a journal can be a helpful tool to allow you to identify your habits, pinpoint your triggers, and work through your emotions. This isn't a food log. It's a journal designed to help you write out why you ate what you ate. Doing this repeatedly will help you recognize your triggers in the present moment and enable you to make better decisions in the future. Some examples of triggers are eating in front of the TV or at the computer, the smell of certain foods, seeing food advertisements, family or social settings where food is served or offered, and a certain time of day. Don't forget to assess emotional triggers such as boredom, loneliness, frustration, and anger. There can be many more, so be on the lookout for them.

Anchor Yourself to Truth and Feed on God's Word

So then, let us not be like others, who are asleep, but let us be awake and sober.

—1 Thess. 5:6

Eat at regular intervals. If you have a history of dieting or deprivation, aim to eat three balanced meals and two nourishing snacks each day. Dieting can backfire. What starts as control often ends in bingeing or compulsive eating. Focus on nutrient-dense foods that offer a mix of vitamins, minerals, antioxidants, fiber, complex carbohydrates, healthy fats, and protein. *Tip:* Include protein with every meal. It helps you feel fuller longer, stabilizes blood sugar, and helps balance your hormones, which can reduce the risk of developing insulin resistance (see Chapter 2).

Anchor Yourself to Truth and Feed on God's Word

For he satisfies the thirsty and fills the hungry with good things.

—Ps. 107:9

Make friends with fiber. Fiber is a simple but powerful way to support balanced eating. It helps us feel full after meals, keeps digestion regular, and plays a key role in balancing blood-sugar levels. You can find fiber in plant-based foods—fruits, veggies, whole grains, legumes, nuts, seeds—and it comes in two forms: soluble (dissolves in water) and insoluble (it doesn't). Fiber plays an important supporting role, working behind the scenes to keep everything running smoothly. As you begin to add more fiber-rich foods to your diet, remember this important tip: Fiber needs water to do its job well. Without enough fluids, it can leave you feeling bloated or backed up.

Anchor Yourself to Truth and Feed on God's Word

Then God said, "I give you every seed-bearing plant on the face of the whole earth and every tree that has fruit with seed in it. They will be yours for food."
—Gen. 1:29

Take responsibility for your food choices and eating habits. You can't always choose your circumstances, but you can always choose how you respond. Taking responsibility for your choices helps you become more mindful of your behavior. Recognize where you need to make some changes and let go of the excuses. But ditch the criticism and judgment. Next time, choose the response that aligns with your healthy eating goals.

Anchor Yourself to Truth and Feed on God's Word

It is for freedom that Christ has set us free. Stand firm, then, and do not let yourselves be burdened again by a yoke of slavery.
—Gal. 5:1

Cultivating Mindfulness in the Present Moment

We learned a lot in the previous Be Mindful chapter about how our thoughts influence our behavior. Just as you can pause to discern where a thought is coming from, you can apply a similar technique to your eating habits. If uncontrollable cravings continuously sabotage your healthy eating resolve, pause and assess what emotions you are feeling before you reach for that comfort food. Remember, we want to bring unconscious beliefs to awareness. Are you reaching for the bag of chocolate-covered almonds while you're working because you crave something sweet or because you're anxious about a task you need to accomplish? Once you determine why you want to eat the treat, you'll be able to consciously decide whether you actually need to eat it. (Craving something sweet can be a sign of a blood-sugar imbalance. Remember that eating nutrient-dense food at regular intervals can help minimize these cravings.)

Let Jesus become the One you turn to when you're tempted to turn to unhealthy eating or dieting behaviors. Let Him feed you with His Word and be your stable foundation to stand on when the storms of life try to bring you down.

Now that we've learned how to cultivate stable conditions through Christ and balanced eating, it's time to learn about the second way we can Be Kind to ourselves.

Forgiveness of the Past

We can Be Kind to ourselves by letting go of any criticism from past diet failures, disordered eating, or episodes of starving, binging, or just plain habitual emotional eating. We need to let go of the accusation that we are helpless and out of control and can never make peace with food or ourselves for that matter. These are lies designed to keep us stuck, making us feel like we'll never live up to perfection or what society deems acceptable. We have a kind, loving, and forgiving God who sees our imperfections and failures and still loves us no matter what.

> *We have a kind, loving, and forgiving God who sees our imperfections and failures and still loves us no matter what.*

> *So now there is no condemnation for those who belong to Christ Jesus. And because you belong to him, the power of the life-giving Spirit has freed you from the power of sin that leads to death.*
>
> —Rom. 8:1–2 NLT

How Is Kindness Defined?

To Be Kind is to be generous, helpful, and thinking of other people's feelings ("The Meaning of Kind in English" 2024). It can also be known as having the following qualities: warmheartedness, tenderheartedness, goodwill, affectionateness, concern, and care.

What does it mean to Be Kind to yourself? Could it be done by caring for and nurturing your body or by showing yourself some compassion during a difficult situation? Could being kind be about being gentle and tenderhearted toward ourselves when we suffer, fail, or feel inadequate rather than ignoring our pain or inflicting self-criticism? I think so. "Therefore, as God's chosen people, holy and dearly loved, clothe yourselves with compassion, kindness, humility, gentleness and patience" (Col. 3:12).

Just as kindness exhibits tenderness, warmheartedness, care, and concern, do you know what the opposite of kindness does? It exhibits intolerance, mercilessness, harshness, meanness, and even hatred. If God doesn't want us to act this way toward others, what makes it okay to act this way toward ourselves? It doesn't. I believe it is pleasing to God when we are kind and gentle with ourselves. That includes balancing our food choices and emotions, letting go of guilt and condemnation, and forgiving ourselves of unrealistic perfection standards. When we anchor ourselves to Jesus, we no longer need to ride the waves of guilt and condemnation. Instead, we can be steadfast in exhibiting mercy, love, compassion, and forgiveness toward ourselves, just as Jesus does the same toward us.

> *When we anchor ourselves to Jesus, we no longer need to ride the waves of guilt and condemnation.*

Let the Truth Sink In

If we confess our sins, he is faithful and just to forgive us our sins and to cleanse us from all unrighteousness.
—1 John 1:9 ESV

Let's pray.

Dear Heavenly Father,

Thank You for Your unlimited kindness and mercy. Please forgive me for not being kind to myself with my eating and dieting (fill in your own words) habits. Help me navigate through the storms and my emotions by being anchored to You and trusting You as the Captain of my life. You alone provide me with everything I need, emotionally and spiritually. Your love is unrestrained and unconditional. Your loving kindness restores my soul. Help me seek You when I feel unbalanced rather than turning to food, diets, or harmful behaviors. Give me the knowledge and wisdom to recognize wise choices and help me make them. And just as You forgive me, help me forgive myself. Thank You. In Jesus's name, amen.

Restoring the Body

Let's forge ahead with a healthy relationship with food. There are so many ways we can learn to embrace food as nourishment and for enjoyment when our stability in Jesus helps balance our choices. Let's begin to view food as a gift from God instead of a curse on our hips. Here's how.

Get curious about food. Explore. Research. Have fun. Where do different fruits, vegetables, and grains come from? How are they grown and in which parts of the world? How many varieties exist within each food family, and what are their unique flavors, textures, and scents? What health benefits do they offer? Let your curiosity lead the way. (Bonus: If you're a teacher, this could make for a pretty awesome lesson plan.)

Embrace diversity. How do other cultures enjoy the foods you love? Can you find new recipes or unique ways to prepare them? What kitchen hacks or cooking techniques might you learn from around the world? Are there interesting stories behind a certain dish or ingredient, like who first discovered it, how it was originally prepared, or how it made its way to North America (or your home country)? Let food be your passport. It's a fun way to travel the world without leaving your kitchen.

Cultivate new taste buds. Explore new herbs, spices, coffees, and teas. How can you incorporate more flavor and variety into your daily meals? Can you make your own herbal teas? What makes for a truly great cup of coffee or tea? Are there local shops that offer tastings or specialty blends? (Hint: Nespresso shops at the mall often do, and hey, if you see George Clooney, tell him I sent you.)

Become your own farmer. Try growing your own fruits, vegetables, or herbs. What recipes can you make from the fresh flavors of your garden? If you're already growing, how can you share your harvest with others? Would you be willing to teach someone how to plant their own garden? Maybe even start a YouTube channel and share what you learn along the way.

Create a themed meal. Set the mood with simple table decor and invite family or friends to gather around the table. Follow Jesus's example of sharing meals. These times nourish both body and soul. You might plan a cozy dinner, a picnic, or a weekend brunch. Feel free to include healthy dishes alongside a few indulgent treats. There's no need for extremes when your foundation is steady. And don't stress the details. A casual taco night or colorful bento boxes can be just as fun and meaningful.

Conclusion

What a blessing it is that God gave us food. Sometimes when I'm being silly, I imagine what it might have been like in the beginning when God created everything. I mean seriously, how did He come up with the idea of food and the abundance of variety? My curious mind wonders perhaps that it went down something like this in Genesis.

God, standing around with one hand on His hip and the other scratching His head: "Hmm, how can I nourish these humans? I know. I'll provide them with food to eat. And just because I can, I'll make sure every palette can be satisfied."

My mouth waters just thinking about all the variety and possibilities. And then my mind races to the New Testament and I think of Jesus sitting around eating bread.

Me: "Jesus, what was your favorite type of food?" I pause briefly and then say, "You must have eaten more than just bread, fish, and figs, right?"

I'm grinning from ear to ear.

At this point, I'm not sure if God is smiling at me or thinks He should have given me more brain cells. But all kidding aside, let's honor the Lord with what He's given us to enjoy, and I'll save my questions for when I get to heaven.

Review and Key Insights to Remember

- Be Kind refers to two things. (1) Avoid all dieting and eating extremes. (2) Let go of guilt and condemnation. Forgive yourself for past dieting and unhealthy eating behaviors.

- Restriction and deprivation create more weight problems in the long term because they sabotage your relationship with food and your body.
- Stability is found by anchoring yourself to Jesus when life circumstances become challenging. Jesus fulfills all our emotional and spiritual needs better than any food or diet can. Ask Him for help.
- Use the Be Mindful techniques in the previous chapter to pause and assess what emotions you are feeling before you restrict or reach for food.
- Balanced eating involves learning to identify what healthy eating looks like for you in order to sustain a lifelong healthy relationship with food, your body, your mind, and your spirit.

Your Surprise Package Has Arrived!

This is one of my favorite go-to meals when time is tight. It's quick, easy to make, and strikes that perfect balance of light yet satisfying. And yes, it's absolutely delicious.

Portobello Mushrooms with Herbed Goat Cheese and Greens

Prep Time: 10 minutes
Bake/Grill Time: 15–20 minutes
Servings: 2

Ingredients:

2 large portobello mushrooms
Coconut oil for spraying
6 oz. herbed goat cheese, divided (room temperature is best for spreading onto mushrooms)
1 small to medium head of butter lettuce, washed and torn into bite-sized pieces
½ red pepper, deseeded and diced
½ yellow pepper, deseeded and diced
½ orange pepper, deseeded and diced
1 tbsp. raw pumpkin seeds
1 tbsp. raw sesame seeds
2 tbsp. hulled hemp seeds

Optional: Handful of arugula or baby spinach, washed (I like to mix this in with the butter lettuce)

Dressing:
- 3 tbsp. extra virgin olive oil
- 1 tbsp. balsamic vinegar
- ½ tbsp. Dijon mustard
- Pinch of Himalayan salt
- Pinch of black pepper
- Pinch of fresh or dried parsley

Directions:

Preheat oven to 350°F. Wash and gently pat dry the portobello mushrooms. Spray with a bit of coconut oil. Place on a baking sheet lined with parchment paper, bake for 5 minutes, and then remove from the oven. Top the mushrooms with goat cheese and return to oven. Bake an additional 8–12 minutes until mushrooms are tender. Grill an additional 1–2 minutes until the cheese starts to turn golden. Remove.

Place lettuce in a large bowl and top with diced peppers and pumpkin, sesame, and hemp seeds. Meanwhile, mix dressing in a small bowl or container. Add to salad when serving. Enjoy!

Chapter 12

Be Beautiful: Those Stinkin' Cowboy Boots

A few years ago, I attended a Christian women's conference. For dinner on the last evening session, all of us were ushered into one large ballroom where round tables were set for 8–10 women. Since everyone was already seated at the table I chose, I introduced myself and waited for the others to do the same. After I got to the fifth person, I jokingly confessed that I probably wouldn't remember everyone's name. And because we had all spent the last two days meeting hundreds of new people, I took the smiles and nods around me as a joke well received. But somehow, I must have offended the woman sitting directly across from me who had just shared her name. She blurted out, "So I should just tell you any name since you won't remember it?" I politely apologized and asked her to repeat her name. After thanking her, she said, rather bluntly, "See, you didn't even realize I just gave you a completely different name." Again, I apologized and said, "It's so loud in here, and it's hard to hear." She smiled and then told me her real name (I'll call her Beverly.)

Once all the names were squared away, we shared which seminars we attended. The seminars had groups of approximately 75-100 women, so when Beverly mentioned she sat in a class I had been in, I said, "Hey, me too! Sorry I didn't see you though." That's when she revealed that she had certainly seen me. Not thinking too much about the comment, I asked her where she was from, and she replied, "Nashville."

"Nashville?" I said excitedly, "I just visited there recently. What a great city you live in." She then asked me if I had purchased the cowboy boots I was wearing in Nashville. Enthusiastically, I answered, "Yes!" And that's when she said, rather condescendingly, "Oh, you bought the tourist boots." Stunned by her remark and unsure if I had heard it correctly, I said, "Pardon me?" A little louder, she repeated, "You bought the tourist boots."

I must have looked confused by her comment because when I didn't respond, she said, "Just kidding. Everyone who comes to Nashville buys cowboy boots. My friends and I joke about it all the time." Again, I froze like a deer in headlights as agonizing seconds ticked by. Finally, I snapped out of it, smiled, and turned to talk to the women next to me.

Throughout dinner and our evening session, shock and hurt took hold of my emotions. As much as I tried to focus on what the keynote speaker was saying, I couldn't get Beverly's comments out of my mind.

My inner dialogue was racing. *Did she really just say that to me? Did I somehow offend her by jokingly admitting that I probably wouldn't remember her name? Did I sound self-important? No way, that's so not who I am. Others admitted to having the same dilemma. Plus, I apologized. Maybe she was angry. I didn't know she was in the same seminar class as I was. Was I rude or indignant in some way? I don't think so. How am I supposed to remember everyone in an entire class of new people? Am I just being overly sensitive here?*

BE BEAUTIFUL: THOSE STINKIN' COWBOY BOOTS

Pause.

No! I heard her correctly. She just made fun of me in front of an entire table filled with other women. She obviously has some issue with me or the way I look because apparently, she had noticed me even before I met her. She made a point of making me feel foolish for not remembering her name in front of the others. Then she had the nerve to insult my choice of footwear as well!

This played in my mind like a broken record until finally, when genuine hurt settled in, I thought, *How could a woman who was at a Christian conference behave this way to another Christian?*

I wrestled with this thought for a few minutes. Then I decided I was going to show her. Once the evening session was over, I would walk right up to her and say her name (because after that comment, I certainly did remember it), and I would tell her what she said was hurtful but that as a fellow sister, I would forgive her.

Yes, this was me taking the high road. I was going to rise above her and smother her with kindness—and secretly make her feel bad for what she said.

Except . . . I couldn't lie to her.

As much as I wanted to have my say and then forgive and forget, I still felt pretty insulted. I knew it wouldn't be right for me to pretend to be the better person when, let's face it, I really wasn't. Because when Beverly said those hurtful things, I began to judge her too. *"Oh, she must have some real self-esteem issues to put someone down like that in front of others."*

The truth is that I didn't know Beverly any more than she knew me. I couldn't make assumptions about her character and who she was as a person based on this one encounter, could I? Wouldn't that be just as mean?

I sat with those thoughts and questions for a couple of minutes until finally I had a chat with God. "Lord, I'm going to assume she didn't really mean to sound the way she did. It's been a long day, and maybe she was just tired. I won't go over and make that fake speech to her, but maybe You could just give her a nudge to come and apologize to me. Then I could forgive her. Yes, I'll wait to see if she approaches me after the evening session."

She never did. So I slowly packed my bags and left the room.

I'd like to tell you my encounter with Beverly has a follow-up happy ending, but unfortunately that's not the case. Me and my cowboy boots left the conference with hurt feelings and a convicted heart.

So why am I telling you this story? Because if this story isn't great material for a teen soap, I don't know what is! But seriously, all kidding aside, it's because Be Beautiful isn't about what you look like. Be Beautiful is about your character—the way you view and treat others and the way you view and treat yourself. True beauty is found within because God doesn't judge beauty the way we do. He judges beauty by looking at the condition of our hearts. But before we dive into learning about His beauty perspective, let's talk about the perspective we are all too familiar with—the way the world views beauty.

Eye candy: A person or thing regarded as superficially pleasing or attractive to look at ("Eye Candy Definition" 2024).

When it comes to beauty, why do we as a society place so much emphasis on how we look? I mean, seriously, do you know that the beauty and personal care market is projected to generate revenue of $677 billion in 2025? ("Beauty & Personal Care - Worldwide" 2024). It seems unbelievable, doesn't it? I know firsthand the amount of money women will spend in their pursuit to look younger and feel more beautiful.

Many years ago, I worked at a skin care company selling beauty products such as anti-aging serums, the latest wrinkle-reducing lotions, and the ever-exclusive-skin-tightening-miracle-in-a-bottle stuff. It all sold like hotcakes despite being incredibly expensive. We women care so much about our outward appearance that we're willing to spend an insane amount of money to try just about anything promising to turn back the hands of time and lead us to the fountain of youth.

And don't even get me started with all the latest fad diets, whether it's no sugar, nonfat, no carbs, high fat, no meat, just fish, a juice fast, or intermittent fasting. You name it, and it's been done. (You mean to tell me this diet will make me look thinner and younger? Sign me up!) We jump into the latest fitness craze—HIIT, Barre, Zumba, and everything in between. Or we scroll TikTok for whatever's trending, hoping it will help us shake off the jiggle in the places we don't like. We invest in home gyms, Pelotons, and the newest high-tech wearables. And let's be honest. Some of us have even fallen for gadgets like the ThighMaster or the Gut Buster. If those names don't ring a bell, do yourself a favor and google them. You'll see what I mean.

But it doesn't stop there. We look for clothes that make us look thinner, taller, and even more glamorous—enter Spanx, high heels, fashion jewelry, and shoulder pads (seriously, how was that ever a good look?). And it's not just women—men often feel self-conscious, too, whether it's about their height, developing "man boobs," or losing their hair. Yet even with all our skin care rituals, fad diets, new workouts, and the most flattering clothes money can buy, we remain unfulfilled and unhappy with our appearance and look to plastic surgery, Botox, and other face- and body-changing methods to affirm we're beautiful. Though we place so much emphasis on our outward appearance, it's the one thing guaranteed to change as we get older. No matter what you do, you can't stop the aging process. So why do we try so hard to be beautiful?

Before you roll your eyes at me, hear me out. I'm not saying it's wrong to want to look our best, have fewer wrinkles, or wear a smaller size. Heaven knows I'm that gal. I own Spanx. I wear heels. I love fashion jewelry. And yes, I had a ThighMaster, a Gut Buster, and a Cindy Crawford exercise video (I'm only a little embarrassed). It's not the pursuit of these beauty tools that's the problem; it's the priority given to them and our misplaced view of what true beauty really is.

Think about it.

Have you ever experienced any of the following?

- You have a favorite outfit you love wearing. But the moment someone makes a negative comment, suddenly you're second-guessing it, wondering if it's been fooling you this whole time.
- Your husband took a picture of you, and you asked to see it before he posted it on social media. He took it from the bottom up. Delete! Try again from a more flattering angle. Bottom down, husbands. Bottom down!
- You wake up in the morning and ever so gently step on the scale—naked, holding your breath so you don't move. The minute you're up a few pounds, it feels like a catastrophic natural disaster. But when you're down a few? The clouds part, a beam of light shines, and angels sing hallelujah!
- You walk into the salon feeling invisible, like even your reflection has stopped trying. But after a fresh blowout, suddenly everyone's smiling, complimenting you, and holding doors like you just won an award.
- When your skin is pale, everyone insists you look tired, like you've been burning the midnight oil for weeks. But the minute you get a tan? Suddenly you're glowing with health like you've been sipping coconut water on a sunny beach.

- Someone made a comment about your turned-up nose, big teeth, thick thighs, big butt, uneven toes, or small boobs, and suddenly all your flaws feel magnified. Or maybe it was a joke about your accent or your ethnicity. Either way, it sticks with you.

I've been the recipient of all these and more. While it's easy to let these kinds of judgments and perceptions, whether good or bad, shape how we see ourselves, we can't allow them to take root in our hearts because they aren't based on truth.

The reality is that the world's view of beauty and what it means to be beautiful—or eye candy—is subjective. It's like building your home on sand, causing it to constantly shift and change. So if we anchor our self-worth and beliefs of what it means to be beautiful on such an unsteady foundation, then it's no wonder we'll never be satisfied.

The only solid foundation and true way to look at beauty is to see it the way God does.

Restoring the Soul

In 1 Samuel 15 when Saul was the King of Israel, the Lord asked Samuel, a prophet, to anoint the next King of Israel. Samuel looked at a possible candidate, Eliab, who, according to the text, was pretty good-looking. Here's what happened.

> *But the LORD said to Samuel, "Do not consider his appearance or his height, for I have rejected him. The LORD does not look at the things people look at. People look at the outward appearance, but the LORD looks at the heart."*
> —1 Sam. 16:7

In this passage of scripture, God told Samuel not to choose the candidate Eliab based on his physical attributes. Instead, the Lord wanted Samuel to consider what really mattered: his inner character.

God doesn't want you or me to judge others by appearance alone because we may overlook what's truly inside their heart. Our appearance doesn't reveal who we are or what we are really like. Only God can accurately see inside us, judging us by faith and character. So while we spend hours each week maintaining our outward appearance, are we giving the same amount of attention to developing our inner self?

> *Our appearance doesn't reveal who we are or what we are really like.*

I know I don't sound beautiful when I speak harshly, raise my voice, gossip, or make a snide comment. I know I wasn't being beautiful when I wanted to call out Beverly at the conference. Even though she never knew what I thought of her in that moment, God certainly did. And I'm pretty sure He didn't think I was being beautiful in that moment.

So how does God look at beauty? Maybe 1 Peter can shed some light on that.

> *Do not let your adorning be external—the braiding of hair and putting on of gold jewelry, or the clothing you wear—but let your adorning be the hidden person of the heart with the imperishable beauty of a gentle and quiet spirit, which in God's sight is very precious.*
>
> —1 Pet. 3:3-4 ESV

What Peter is saying in this passage is that women should develop inner beauty rather than being overly concerned with their outward appearance. We're even told in Proverbs 31:30 that it's important to develop an inner spirit of godliness.

But friend, please don't misunderstand. I am not suggesting that we can't strive to look our best, and God is not saying that either. Our loving Heavenly Father is telling us what matters most, that what takes priority isn't the outward, external appearance but the internal appearance—the condition of the heart. True beauty, the kind that doesn't change and wither with time, is found in a heart that pursues Christ.

> *True beauty, the kind that doesn't change and wither with time, is found in a heart that pursues Christ.*

In contrast, what are we thinking about others when we make assumptions and judgments based on the color of their hair, the wrinkles on their face, or their choice of footwear? (Sorry, I couldn't help myself.) What about when we overlook someone's snide behavior because they fit the look? (Have you ever dated a not-so-nice guy because he was so hot?) What we're saying is that being beautiful on the outside is important. In fact, what we're saying with a megaphone is that external beauty is more important than internal beauty. We're communicating that we judge an individual's self-worth and value based on their appearance—eye candy.

We continue this same unspoken dialogue when we covet someone else's beauty. Have you ever said to yourself, "I wish I had legs like her. I wish I were thin like so and so. I wish I had a flat stomach. I wish, I wish, I wish." I know I have. An "I wish" comment might seem innocent, and I believe it's possible to genuinely appreciate how another woman looks, but there's also a danger zone when our thoughts might sound like this: "I wish I had legs like her, but I was born with tree-stump thighs. I wish I were thin like so and so because she can eat whatever she wants and never gain a pound, unlike me. I wish I had a flat stomach like her, but I hear she got gastric bypass surgery to look like that." This type of self-talk and gossip only continues with the false belief that it's okay to be judged for our appearance rather than how we love, speak, and act. It reinforces the misconception that it's okay to judge, compare, and gossip, and I'm pretty sure the Bible tells us otherwise.

In John 7:24, Jesus says, "Stop judging by mere appearances, but instead judge correctly." It would be easy to read that one line of scripture and think that Jesus is talking about our physical appearance. But if you read the scriptures preceding it, John 7:21–23, you learn that Jesus is talking to a crowd of people who are judging Him for healing on the Sabbath.

This is an important distinction because here we learn that making judgments about someone shouldn't be based on our assumptions of what we think is true but rather on what we know is true. In order to do that, we must realize the only source of truth in this world comes from God, not the constantly changing, ever-shifting, fickle views of this world. Only when we establish our foundation in His infallible Word can we shift our worldview of beauty to His view. This shift enables us to see others (and ourselves) with love instead of judgment, making the boundaries to beauty endless.

I realize, though, that the topic of seeing beauty in everyone isn't exactly a new concept. There have been countless television shows and movies based on judging beauty through a different lens, like the blockbuster hits *Barbie*, *I Feel Pretty*, *Cinderella*, and *Beauty and the Beast*, to name a few. But even with all the media coverage and new faces and body types gracing the covers of our magazines, have we really progressed? It's like society is saying, "Yes, people! We agree we need to be more accepting of all body shapes and sizes and how we define beauty." But the stigma if you don't fit the bill hasn't left us just yet. And if I'm completely honest, sometimes I really do just wish I were a few years younger, a few pounds lighter, and had a few less wrinkles.

So why do we continue to fall into the same trap of feeling inadequate, self-conscious, and judgmental? It's because with as much progress as the world is making, society still isn't perfect. Take one look at any reality TV show, and you'll see women pitted against each other left, right, and center. Sometimes all it takes is one comment from some stranger to change a healthy perception of ourselves to one that is destructive.

Hurtful comments can leave us with a lifelong false impression of who we are. That false impression becomes imprinted in our minds until we believe that's all we are. These imprints damage our health by minimizing and sometimes even paralyzing the beautiful women God created us to be, and we must refuse to take ownership of this deception. That's why it's crucial to Be Mindful of what we think and believe about ourselves and others, and why it's important to Be Kind to ourselves and one another.

> *Hurtful comments can leave us with a lifelong false impression of who we are.*

Our words have the power to build someone up or tear someone down. Words are like weapons that can cause deep wounds and lasting scars. That's why we must be vigilant in protecting the way we use them. The Bible says, "Do not let any unwholesome talk come out of your mouths, but only what is helpful for building others up according to their needs, that it may benefit those who listen" (Eph. 4:29).

Case in point: When I was in elementary school, a friend told me I had a big butt. And just like that, the comment stuck. For years I carried it around like an anchor strapped to my waist. I'd twist and turn in every three-way mirror, trying to catch a glimpse from every angle and always cringing at what I saw. Honestly, sometimes I felt like that's who I was—the girl with the big butt. Fast forward a few years, and to my total surprise it suddenly became cool to have what we now call a booty. Jeans were being marketed to lift, sculpt, and boost what I was trying to hide. And the best part? I didn't need them. These days, when I catch myself wondering if it's still too big, God has a way of using that mirror to remind me that my value runs a lot deeper than my rear-end real estate.

Action Step: Write the following scriptures on some sticky notes and put them on your mirrors all around your house. Keep some on your phone for emergencies.

Let the Truth Sink In

Charm is deceptive, and beauty is fleeting; but a woman who fears the Lord is to be praised.
—Prov. 31:30

One thing I ask from the Lord, this only do I seek: that I may dwell in the house of the Lord all the days of my life, to gaze on the beauty of the Lord and to seek him in his temple.
—Ps. 27:4

The grass withers, the flower fades, but the word of our God will stand forever.
—Isa. 40:8 ESV

You are altogether beautiful, my darling; there is no flaw in you.
—Song of Songs 4:7

I praise you because I am fearfully and wonderfully made; your works are wonderful, I know that full well.
—Ps. 139:14

Let's pray.

Dear Heavenly Father,

I praise You for Your Word, which is edifying and encouraging. Thank You for loving me so much that You care about how I feel about my appearance. You know my deepest struggles and concerns. Please forgive me for coveting, gossiping, judging (insert your own words). Show me how to develop more inner godliness and focus less on my so-called flaws. Help me in the areas concerned with the attitude of my heart and character. Remind me not to judge myself or others and to take care of myself as an act of worship, not as an act of vanity. I adore You for ministering your truth to my heart. In Jesus's name, amen.

Restoring the Body

Okay, now that we have talked about how to Be Beautiful, let's explore other aspects of beauty on the inside. And yes, I mean your physical insides, particularly your organs, your digestive system, and even your bowel movements.

You may be wondering how we can explore the physical beauty of our inside or, more importantly, why we should focus on this kind of internal beauty. It's because you, my friend, were formed by the hands of our Creator, and He gave you a body designed to function in a particular way. We honor God's divine design by easing the process of digestion, supporting the organs with powerhouse nutrients, and ultimately having really good poops. Let's take a closer look, shall we?

What Goes In Must Come Out

When it comes to digestion, it's important to remember that we want the body to effectively process the good stuff (nutrients from the food we consume) and efficiently eliminate the bad stuff (waste) in a timely manner. But before we get to what to do, let's learn how the digestion system works ("Your Digestive System and How It Works" 2017).

The process of digestion starts before food even enters your mouth. The glands in your mouth begin to pump out saliva when you anticipate food, like when cooking a meal or looking at a menu. Once food enters your mouth, a special enzyme in your saliva helps break down food as you chew.

As food moves down your esophagus and into your stomach, hormones trigger the release of acids and enzyme-rich juices that break down food, turning it into a soupy substance called chyme. These hormones also signal the pancreas, liver, and gallbladder to produce digestive juices and transfer bile (a liquid that digests fat) to your small intestine to prepare for the next stage.

The chyme enters the small intestine (gut) where fats, proteins, and carbohydrates are broken down into nutrients. Your intestinal wall is lined with millions of tiny projections called villi that increase the surface area for nutrient absorption. Nutrients are then transferred into the bloodstream, feeding organs and tissues and leaving waste behind.

The waste (undigested fiber, water, and dead cells) proceeds to the large intestine (colon) where most of the remaining fluid is absorbed in order to produce stool.[11] Stool is then squeezed into the rectum until we feel the need to poop. We head to the toilet, and ta-daaa! That's digestion from beginning to end—literally.

Now that we know how the digestive system works, we can offer support by helping it along. But how do you know if it needs help? The body gives us many clues. Do you experience constant bloating, gas, or water retention? Do you suffer from heartburn, indigestion, or constipation? Do you rely on laxatives to go to the bathroom? Do you have fewer than one bowel movement a day? Do you suffer from chronic yeast infections? These are all indicators that your digestive system is working overtime and could use a little help. And it doesn't stop there.

Poor digestion leads to toxic overload (recall Chapter 2.) Those toxins will look for other ways to exit the body such as through your beautiful-looking skin. How? Are you suffering from acne or

---

[11] The small and large intestines contain trillions of strains of bacteria and microbes that help our digestion and keep our immune system strong and healthy.

dry, itchy, flaky skin? Does your hair look dull, or has it lost its shine? Do your nails break easily? Do you have dark circles under your eyes? These are just a few of the many ways our body talks to us through symptoms.

When we focus on Being Beautiful on the inside, our outside also reaps the rewards. Here are a few simple ways we can help our digestion and look (and feel) better.

How to Improve the Digestive Process

- Start your day by drinking a cup of hot water with freshly squeezed lemon juice before you drink anything else. It's a gentle liver detox and can help move things along.
- Slow down, missy! Eating too fast can lead to an upset stomach and portion distortion. Eat slowly until you are satiated, but don't overeat. That can cause bloating, flatulence, and indigestion, not to mention eating way more than you need.
- Chew your food thoroughly. Your stomach will thank you for all the chomping when you send a mushy paste down your pipe as opposed to large, half-chewed mouthfuls.
- Drink plenty of water between meals, but avoid large quantities of liquids with your meals. They dilute those important digestive juices and enzymes that work so hard to break down food in your tummy.
- Eat more fiber-rich foods. I know, I've mentioned fiber before, but it's worth repeating because it plays such a key role in digestion. Fiber helps us feel full longer, and it acts as a scrub, brushing away waste from the wall of the colon and absorbing potentially harmful toxins. Some of my favorite sources are apples, avocados, celery, cauliflower, broccoli, pears, and kale.

- Consider supplementing with probiotics. The balance of good versus bad bacteria is critical for healthy digestion, nutrient absorption, and our immune system. A poor diet, antibiotics, birth control pills, and certain medications can alter the balance of good to bad bacteria, leading to leaky gut syndrome (Chapter 2) and a slew of other health issues.

Here are two things you can do to learn more about the health of your digestive system.

Get the Scoop on Poop![12]

1. Have a look at your poop on a regular basis. Seriously! I know how this sounds. But knowing what your poop looks like when it's normal (it should be light to medium brown, S- or C-shaped, and not extremely foul-smelling) will help you recognize when your digestion might need some extra attention.
2. Do the beet test. Wash, peel, and grate some raw red beets into a salad or roast them (make my Roasted Beet and Pistachio Salad, Chapter 8). Don't use fermented beets because they won't have the same effect. After you've eaten the beets, note the date and time, then check your stool and record when you first notice a red color. Don't be alarmed. The red is from the beets. Optimal bowel transit time is 12–24 hours, so if you see the beets before that, your body may not be absorbing nutrients effectively, leading to malabsorption. If fecal matter sits too long in your gut, you're dealing with constipation. To have beautiful insides and a nice-looking outside, incorporate one or more of the following suggestions:

---

[12] I actually wrote an article about poop. Read it at https://www.thelocalbizmagazine.ca/archives/LB201901-WEB.pdf (Schaefer 2019).

- Consume plenty of dark, leafy greens rich in vitamin K, which helps prevent collagen loss, thereby improving skin elasticity. Enjoy spinach, kale, collard greens, brussels sprouts, chards, spirulina, and wheatgrass, just to name a few.
- Eat and drink your antioxidants found in berries, brightly colored veggies, and green tea. Antioxidants protect your cells against the effects of cellular damage and free radicals that can cause disease and premature aging.
- Drink green juices, and fresh is best. Green juices are a wonderful way to boost hydration and elevate energy levels.
- Incorporate dry-skin brushing or shower hydrotherapy (alternating between hot and cold water temps). Both are a great way to stimulate circulation and improve skin tone with a beautiful, natural, rosy complexion.
- I don't want to keep hammering these points, but if you reduce your stress levels, sleep 7-9 hours per night, and drink at least two to three liters of filtered water per day, you'll not only reap all the benefits I've mentioned previously, but you'll look better too.

Conclusion

Every woman wants to feel beautiful, no matter how young or old they are. Though Be Beautiful is about how we can focus on our character and insides, let's not forget how beautiful it is to be kind to someone else. Many older women struggle with their aging body and appearance. Next time you see your mom, gram, or elderly friend, tell her how beautiful she looks. It might be the only nice thing she's heard all day.

Review and Key Insights to Remember

- Be Beautiful is about developing your character—the way you view and treat others and the way you view and treat yourself.
- God is the only One who can accurately judge our character and heart.
- Gossiping about, coveting, or judging others' appearance is not beautiful and only continues to fuel a false perception of who you truly are.
- Beauty is found in a heart that pursues Christ.
- Good digestion helps you look beautiful both inside and out.

Your Surprise Package Has Arrived!

Do you want silky, radiant skin without spending a fortune on skin care products? Try dry skin brushing, a simple practice that boosts circulation, sloughs off dead skin cells, and stimulates the lymphatic system to support detoxification. And it leaves your skin feeling soft, smooth, and refreshed.

Your Go-To Guide to Dry-Skin Brushing

What you need:
A natural-bristle, medium-soft brush, preferably with a long handle for hard-to-reach spots

When to do it:
Before you shower

How to do it:
Lower body: Gently but firmly, using small strokes, brush your skin starting at the bottom of the feet and working your way up your legs. Continue brushing up the torso toward the heart.

Upper body: Start at your hands and brush up your arms, always sweeping up toward your heart. From the neck, brush down toward the heart. Be sure not to press too hard as skin may be sensitive in certain areas. *Note:* Dry-skin brushing should not hurt.

How often to do it: Dry-skin brushing can be done 3–5 times per week.

Chapter 13

Believe: Call Me by My Name

Go anywhere where people don't know you, and if you don't like something about yourself, you have the opportunity to change it. I learned this little trick at a very young age—five years old, to be exact. You see, in all those five years I had been alive, I had come to really despise my name. That's because the name Bianca was not as common as it is today. And because it was uncommon, I was often asked to repeat myself a little louder. Of course, that always set off the predictable questions that would follow—"Where are you from? What's your ethnicity?"—to which I found my five-year-old self growing more and more self-conscious with each new introduction.

Sometimes I was teased about my name because it was different. But I suppose it wasn't just my name I became anxious about. Just mentioning I was German often prompted racial slurs that I couldn't quite understand at the time. Suffice it to say that being an immigrant in Canada with an uncommon name was not something I was proud of. (Unfortunately, my rye bread and liverwurst sandwiches didn't help my situation either, but that's a story for another time.) The point is that being a Bianca just wasn't worth all the trouble that came along with it. Time and time again, I caught myself thinking, "Why couldn't I just have a normal name?"

That's why when we moved to a new city where I met some kids playing on the street, I decided to take matters into my own hands and proudly introduce myself as Michelle. To me, Michelle sounded very Canadian and seemed like the perfect name to help me blend in. Finally, my life was going to change for the better.

A couple hours after meeting my new friends, one of their moms came outside to check on us. Not knowing who I was, she bent down and asked me, "What's your name?" And without even thinking, I replied, "Bianca." One of the other kids blurted out quickly, "I thought you said your name was Michelle." As my head hung low and my cheeks turned several shades of pink (and all time stood still), I embarrassingly confessed that my name was not Michelle but was indeed Bianca. And that quickly put an end to my newfound identity.

These days, telling people my name is no big deal. I've actually met a few Biancas throughout my lifetime, and I've even come to like my name—all of it, Bianca Christel Schaefer. And the cool thing is, I had no idea how significant a name could be. I've even learned that your name is part of your identity. The question is, do you know who you are?

> "A life without proper identity is a life without joy and peace" (from the movie *Overcomer*) (Kendrick 2019).

In our present day and age, we often define ourselves through our accomplishments or what we do for a living. We identify ourselves as parents or single, married or divorced; as following a certain religion or political party, or even as vegans, athletes, or philanthropists. We think we know who we are based on what we think of ourselves or maybe what we think others expect of us. But when we let ourselves and others define us by these standards, it can often lead to uncertainties, confusion, or disappointment about our self-identity. And God never intended for us to be disappointed, confused, or misled. The truth is that God perfectly designed us because He defined us before we even came into being. He even knows us more intimately than we know ourselves. And He created us with a specific purpose (Ps. 139:1–16).

At the beginning of this book, I mentioned I didn't know who I was in Christ. But the truth is, I'm not sure I really knew who I was at all. We learned in The Unhealthy Body Cycle: Part One that we can develop low self-esteem when we become unhealthy. Remember the cycle? One thing leads to another and another until you second-guess your self-worth—all because you may have gained weight or don't look or feel as healthy as you'd like. Maybe you've even started to identify with being a big person or the overweight friend. The problem is that now your weight or appearance is beginning to define who you are.

Self-esteem is defined as a person's sense of self-worth (Du, King, and Chi 2017). While everyone can lack confidence from time to time, people with low self-esteem feel unsatisfied with themselves most of the time. They can be extremely critical of themselves, judge themselves, use negative words to describe themselves, blame themselves, and may not believe it when someone compliments them. Constant self-criticism leads to persistent feelings of sadness, depression, anxiety, anger, shame, or guilt. They believe they must earn love or friendship. They may lack self-care, neglect themselves, or develop self-harming behaviors such as overeating, alcohol abuse, or substance disorder. They may even doubt their abilities and worth ("Self-Esteem" 2024).

Some causes of low self-esteem can be linked to an unhappy childhood or an extremely critical upbringing. For some, it could have been brought on by poor academic performance in school or poor treatment from a partner, family member, or employer. Or it could stem from mental illness, depression, an anxiety disorder, a chronic illness, or a physical disability.

But low self-esteem doesn't just affect people with a poor upbringing, traumatic experience, or mental or physical illnesses. We can all suffer from self-esteem issues at various stages in our lives, from childhood all the way to senior living.

From The Unhealthy Body Cycle: Part Two, we saw that suffering from low self-esteem can be brought on by a loss of perspective, forgetting we were made in the image of God. We can also develop low self-esteem when we lose sight of how significant we are to God or how much He loves us. Instead, we're bombarded with the constant pressure of how society defines the perfect woman, and in the end, we're so frazzled that it's no wonder we struggle with defining who we are.

The now-famous monologue spoken by actress America Ferrera in the blockbuster movie *Barbie* touches on the exact struggle so many women of our present time battle with—the impossibility of being a woman. Allow me to paraphrase the monologue: One of the biggest struggles women deal with is trying to be a representation of the perfect woman yet never feeling good enough to fill the shoes society demands. It seems that *perfect* means everything from being a great mom to being a successful career woman; to being thin, young, and beautiful to being kind and financially stable, never complaining and having everything in life completely and perfectly in order. And while women are trying to juggle all these things as best they can, they're left feeling like a failure who's disappointed, unacknowledged, and ungrateful.[13]

---

[13] Read the full monologue at https://www.townandcountrymag.com/leisure/arts-and-culture/a44725030/america-ferrera-barbie-full-monologue-transcript/ (Burack 2023).

When I saw this scene in the movie, I nodded in agreement, thinking, *Yeah, finally someone understands the pressures we women feel.* And I could almost see myself wanting to stand up, clap, and organize some kind of rally. But soon after that moment, another thought came to mind, and my heart felt troubled. And here's what I want to share with you.

It's easy to develop low self-esteem when we base our self-worth on anything other than our God-given identity just so others will like us, accept us, approve of us, or look up to us. The only way you'll ever feel good enough is if you know Who is good.

> *It's easy to develop low self-esteem when we base our self-worth on anything other than our God-given identity.*

The book *Defined: Who God Says You Are* says that "(1) . . . knowing our God-given identity is a key priority for each of us, and (2) allowing God to be the One to help us discover it and live it out is foundational to fulfilling our purpose in life" (Kendrick and Kendrick 2019, 11). In other words, knowing who we are helps shape who we become, the decisions we make, and how we ultimately live our lives.

The book *Atomic Habits* says it this way: "Your behaviors are usually a reflection of your identity. What you do is an indication of the type of person you believe that you are—either consciously or nonconsciously. . . . Research has shown that once a person believes in a particular aspect of their identity, they are more likely to act in alignment with that belief" (Clear 2018, 34).

That's why when we suffer from low self-esteem, it cripples who God has purposefully designed us to be and destined us to become. Having healthy self-esteem is exactly what God wants us to maintain in order to live out our lives according to His purpose.

Believe is about developing healthy self-esteem based on your identity in Christ. When you have healthy self-esteem, you can have the confidence to believe in yourself. You must Believe in yourself to make healthy lifestyle changes because when challenges come, remembering your worth will keep you going.

The Bible tells us that God wanted everything He created to have a name and an identity. We do this, too, when we name our children, pets, boats, cars, or the things we have personal relationships with. We identify with names.

So what's in a name? A few Google searches revealed the meanings of my name.

Bianca: white, fair.[14] The definition of *white* is a color that is most complete and pure. The psychological meaning of white is purity, innocence, wholeness, and completion. In color psychology, white is the color of new beginnings, wiping the slate clean so to speak. It is the color with the property of bringing calmness, comfort, and hope.[15]

Now, anyone who knows me well must be laughing at this point because I definitely have not lived a pure, innocent, calm life. But God has always known I'd have a new beginning, that through my faith in Christ, my slate would be wiped clean. So maybe He planted the name Bianca in my mom's head. Grin!

Christel: a Christian, follower of Christ, anointed.[16] Though I was not raised in a Christian home, clearly God had plans for me.

Schaefer: shepherd. It's spelled Schafer with the German spelling, derived from Old High German.[17] Of course, I'm not *the* Shepherd, but I think God has big plans for me—*huge*! (remember *Pretty Woman*?).

---

[14] To find the meaning of Bianca, I used https://charlies-names.com/en/ (2024).
[15] According to Color Psychology at https://www.colorpsychology.org/white/ (Van Braam 2024).
[16] To find the meaning of Christel, I used https://charlies-names.com/en/ (2024).
[17] To find the meaning of Schaefer, I used https://www.ancestry.com/name-origin?surname=schaefer ("Schaefer Family History" 2024).

And there you have it: *Bianca Christel Schaefer*, a name I used to be ashamed of and yet perhaps a name that perfectly defines who God is shaping me to be. Instead of associating my name with unpleasant past experiences, I now choose to view my name as a sweet reminder of how God is always at work in me, refining me to look beyond myself to Him for my self-worth. It's amazing how God can change our perspective on something as trivial as disliking our name.

So, my friend, if you were to google your name, what definition would it have? Would it have an ultra-cool meaning or perhaps something completely unrelatable to you? Don't be discouraged by whatever you find. Though you may identify with your name, don't forget that it's not the sum total of who you are. After all, we can change our names. In fact, God changed many names in the Bible. One example is Jacob, Abraham's grandson. He deceived his father, Isaac, and stole his brother Esau's birthright, a blessing meant for the oldest son, not Jacob. Jacob means supplanter or deceiver. That's not exactly a flattering name. But eventually, it was Jacob's faith that led God to give him the new name, Israel (Gen. 32:28), which means "having power with God."

So why did God change names? In biblical times, a name often referred to the nature, purpose, and makeup of an individual. Perhaps God changed their names to better reflect their purpose on earth. I can't help but reflect on what this is like when we accept Christ as our Lord and Savior. We use the term *born again* to imply a new beginning. The old life has passed away, and the new creation is what we have become in Christ Jesus. And though our earthly name is part of our identity, the Bible tells us that one day we will be given a new name.

> *Whoever has ears, let them hear what the Spirit says to the churches. To the one who is victorious, I will give some of the hidden manna. I will also give that person a white stone with a new name written on it, known only to the one who receives it.*
> —Rev. 2:17

While we may or may not have the name that best suits our identity right now on earth, we can be confident that God knows exactly who we are by our true name, which He has already chosen for us.

Let's shift gears now and get to your identity because it's the things you hold closest in your heart that influence what you believe about yourself and how you behave. In the Bible, anything that takes precedence over worshiping God is defined as an idol. That means the idol is more important than your relationship with Christ. It could be the pursuit of money, beauty, or youth. But it could also be a career, the need for success or adoration, a relationship, or a hobby. And while you may never set out with the intention of worshiping these things, they can easily grow into gods that ultimately control your thoughts and energies. They may be the need to have the perfect body, the perfect family, or the coveted business. Or maybe it's the need to be the one everyone comes to for advice, to have a huge social media following, or to be a highly sought-after speaker, writer, or influencer. These things can all compete for our identity and affect our self-esteem when things don't go according to plan.

Thankfully, we can look to Scripture to learn about who God says we are. The Bible tells us we are loved (John 3:16), we are worthy (Zeph. 3:17), we are blessed (Eph. 1:3), we are purposed (Jer. 29:11), we are called (2 Pet. 1:3), we are gifted (1 Pet. 4:10), we are chosen (1 Pet. 2:9), we are forgiven (Eph. 1:7), we are redeemed (Isa. 43:1), we are wonderfully made (Ps. 139:14), we are made in His image (Gen. 1:27), and we are His children (1 John 3:1).

We can be confident and have self-confidence because of who God says we are in Christ Jesus. That means we can walk with assurance that though we may not yet be all He wants us to be, we can

> *Though we may not yet be all God wants us to be, we can Believe that we will be.*

Believe that we will be. And though society is trying to define who we are by making us believe we need to live up to impossible standards, God takes that burden away from us. Because He is the One loving us, molding us, shaping us, purifying us, being patient with us, forgiving us, and offering His grace, mercy, and kindness. If we trust Him to do the work in us, that's one less thing on our to-do list.

When it comes to your health and life, why is it crucial to Believe in yourself? The reason is that if you don't believe in yourself, you won't have the confidence that you are worth all the effort to have the healthy lifestyle you dream of. And we both know it's easy to feel confident when everything is going smoothly. But the minute there are some bumps in the road, we tend to second-guess ourselves. If you don't truly with all your heart believe you are worth the effort to change your life, you'll backslide. You must Believe in yourself.

> *If you don't believe you are worth the effort to change your life, you'll backslide. You must Believe in yourself.*

Having this self-confidence comes from knowing and truly believing in your identity in Christ. And just to be clear, having self-confidence is not the same as having self-reliance, which is believing and acting as if it all depends on you. Friend, I love you, but no, it doesn't all depend on you, even when it sometimes feels that way. Having true self-confidence is knowing that it all depends on Christ who lives in you, and because of Him, you can be confident and self-assured, and feel good about yourself. Can I get an amen?

Restoring the Soul
Building Self-Confidence
The key to building self-confidence is found in the Word of God. Scripture reminds us of who we are, who God is, and what He is

capable of. Believing in yourself requires faith and action. It requires trust and obedience. Confidence comes when we Believe who God says we are and act like we Believe it. So when you're having one of those days—like when your health journey stalls or your coworker gets the promotion you earned—or when you feel you're failing in everything, don't let these disappointments creep in on your confidence and self-worth. It's all about perspective. If you Believe, you can achieve because you know Who's with you on each step of The B.Losophy Way.

Don't Be Like Moses Before He Was Moses
I've often wondered why the Bible goes into so much detail when we read about Moses's first encounter with God. It's a conversation that starts in Exodus 3 and continues to the end of Exodus 4. And if you're familiar with it, I'm sure you can guess where I'm going with this. Before Moses received the Ten Commandments from God or led the Israelites out of slavery from Egypt, he struggled with his self-confidence. Let's see if there's anything else we can learn. Here's a bit of the back story on how Moses was tasked with being a leader in the first place.

Moses was born an Israelite but raised by the Pharaoh's daughter in Egypt. When he was a grown man, he killed an Egyptian for unjustly beating an Israelite. Fearing he would be killed, Moses took off to Midian (known today as Northeastern Saudi Arabia) where he eventually encountered God in the flames of a burning bush. Curious how the bush could be engulfed in flames without burning up, he approached the bush and heard the voice of God calling him to get closer. That's when God told Moses that He had come to rescue the Israelites from slavery. And here's where we'll jump into the conversation and discover what God says to Moses.

> *"So now, go. I am sending you to Pharaoh to bring my people the Israelites out of Egypt." But Moses said to God, "Who am I that I should go to Pharaoh and bring the Israelites out of Egypt?" And God said, "I will be with you. And this will be the sign to you that it is I who have sent you: When you have brought the people out of Egypt, you will worship God on this mountain." Moses said to God, "Suppose I go to the Israelites and say to them, 'The God of your fathers has sent me to you,' and they ask me, 'What is his name?' Then what shall I tell them?" God said to Moses, "I AM WHO I AM. This is what you are to say to the Israelites: 'I AM has sent me to you.'"*[18]
> —Exod. 3:10–14

But the conversation doesn't stop there. God then tells Moses exactly what to do, who to talk to, and what the plan is. I could go on and on here because the conversation between God and Moses goes back and forth for quite a few passages, so I hope you don't mind that I'm going to paraphrase the rest. (But please do read it for yourself as well in Exodus 3:15–22.)

You see, Moses wasn't exactly thrilled about this God-given task. In fact, he really struggled with self-doubt and felt utterly inadequate for the job. Not only that, but even after God explained the plan, reassured Moses He'd be with Him, gave him two signs, and explained the outcome, Moses was still reluctant. To make a long story short, Moses not only struggled with self-confidence and doubted his ability (he may have had a speech impediment), but the real problem was he didn't Believe in himself. Finally, Moses asked God to find someone else to do it. (Have you ever felt like God

---

[18] I AM is the name God used to identify who He was. It describes His eternal power and unchanging character. By using this name, people would know exactly who Moses was referring to—the one true God, not some other human-invented idol or god.

was tasking you with something you'd rather He asked someone else to do? I know I have.) By this time, God was not too happy with Moses's reluctance. Nevertheless, God told Moses that his brother Aaron could help him with the task and that together, they would both have His support (Exod. 4:1–17).

Throughout this conversation, God teaches us how to place our confidence in Him, not in our perceived flaws. We learn that if He asks us to do something, He has a plan and will give us the support we need to carry it out. Though the task may not be easy, if we trust Him, He won't let us fall. And finally, what God wants, God gets. God had a plan and purpose for Moses's life, just as He has for ours.

If you lack self-confidence, you'll shrivel up in despair. You'll shrink and always second-guess yourself, just like the old Moses. It's like taking one step forward and one step back. You'll get nowhere. Having self-confidence is taking one step forward and having the courage to do it again and again. This kind of self-confidence isn't based on a puffed-up view of how great we are. Let's not be so arrogant to think that because we can achieve, we're better than others. We just need a healthy dose of confidence, enough so we believe we can accomplish our goals and dreams but not so much that we forget Who gets the credit. Capeesh?

Let the Truth Sink In

Action Step: Discover your true self by studying identity scriptures a little more closely. Meditate on them and journal how they resonate with you. What is God teaching you about this aspect of Him and your identity? Keep this journal visibly in sight and reread it often. Make it a point to memorize a few of your favorite identity scriptures. In the chart below are some suggested scriptures. Whenever you are feeling down about yourself, ask the Holy Spirit to help you recall your identity in Christ.

Identity Scriptures		
You Are Loved	John 3:16	For God so loved the world that he gave his one and only Son, that whoever believes in him shall not perish but have eternal life.
You Are Worthy	Zephaniah 3:17	The Lord your God is with you, the Mighty Warrior who saves. He will take great delight in you; in his love he will no longer rebuke you, but will rejoice over you with singing.
You Are Purposed	Jeremiah 29:11	"For I know the plans I have for you," declares the Lord, "plans to prosper you and not to harm you, plans to give you hope and a future."
You Are Called	2 Peter 1:3	His divine power has given us everything we need for a godly life through our knowledge of him who called us by his own glory and goodness.
You Are Chosen	1 Peter 2:9	But you are a chosen people, a royal priesthood, a holy nation, God's special possession, that you may declare the praises of him who called you out of darkness into his wonderful light.
You Are Forgiven	Ephesians 1:7	In him we have redemption through his blood, the forgiveness of sins, in accordance with the riches of God's grace.
You Are Redeemed	Isaiah 43:1	But now, this is what the Lord says—he who created you, Jacob, he who formed you, Israel: "Do not fear, for I have redeemed you; I have summoned you by name; you are mine."
You Are Made in God's Image	Genesis 1:27	So God created mankind in his own image, in the image of God he created them; male and female he created them.
You Are a Child of God	1 John 3:1	See what great love the Father has lavished on us, that we should be called children of God! And that is what we are! The reason the world does not know us is that it did not know him.
You Are Blessed	Ephesians 1:3	Praise be to the God and Father of our Lord Jesus Christ, who has blessed us in the heavenly realms with every spiritual blessing in Christ.
You Are Wonderfully Made	Psalm 139:15–16	My frame was not hidden from you when I was made in the secret place, when I was woven together in the depths of the earth. Your eyes saw my unformed body; all the days ordained for me were written in your book before one of them came to be.
You Are Gifted	1 Peter 4:10	Each of you should use whatever gift you have received to serve others, as faithful stewards of God's grace in its various forms.

Let's pray.

Dear Heavenly Father,

Thank You for the identity You have given me in Christ Jesus. Please forgive me when I have let my fears, doubts, and insecurities cause me to be disobedient to You or to what You ask of me. Father, I know that if I ask according to Your will in Jesus's name, You will give it to me. So, Father, I ask that You help me truly believe who You say I am and to walk by faith and confidence, knowing that I am worthy of all the effort it takes to implement healthy lifestyle changes. Together with You I am capable of transformation. I praise You for the strength and courage You give me with every step throughout this journey. In Jesus's name, amen.

Restoring the Body

For we are God's handiwork, created in Christ Jesus to do good works, which God prepared in advance for us to do.
—Eph. 2:10

Knowing your identity and self-worth is one thing. Now it's time to put your faith into action and Believe in yourself. Here are four things you can do to help fuel your self-confidence tank.

1. **Face your fear head on.** Fear has a way of keeping us stuck. The key to overcoming it is to face it head on. Write a list of your fears and the skills you need to overcome them. For example, let's say this is one of your fears: "What if I put the weight back on once I've lost it?" Writing it out helps us plan a course of action. What skills do you need

or what will you do to keep the weight off? Write down your action plan. Be specific and see how that changes your perspective.

2. **Hire a coach.** Sometimes we lack confidence because we're unsure how to do something. It could be as simple as how to make more plant-based meals (that aren't salads) or more complex such as how to pursue a new career path. Hiring a coach can help you gain clarity, knowledge, and skills. Knowing how to do something more easily or more quickly can help you feel more confident.

3. **Make a phone call.** We all need a little pep talk from time to time. Only someone who truly knows you, loves you, and has your best interest at heart can speak to you like no one else can. When you don't believe in yourself, call the person you trust the most. It could be a pastor, a friend, a mentor, or a loved one. This isn't about asking for advice. Tell them what you're struggling with and that you need some reassurance. Sometimes hearing someone say they believe in you is all you need to Believe in yourself.

4. **Do something you're good at.** This might be a no-brainer, but doing something you're good at helps you feel more confident. And by repeating it, you'll become better at it. Don't say there's nothing you're good at. If you can't think of anything, go ahead and pick up the phone and make that call. You might be surprised by the talents others see in you.

You can also build your self-confidence by challenging yourself to take small leaps of faith. They can target any area in your life where you want to see transformation. From a healthy-living perspective, that means you don't have to implement every suggestion I've outlined in this book all by next week. Take it one step at a time, assessing what works for you and what might need some tweaking in order to achieve lasting results. A friend of mine always said, "Inch by inch, it's a cinch." Becoming more confident is a skill you can learn. When you succeed at achieving one small goal, it gives you the confidence and motivation to do it again. It fuels your self-confidence tank, and you will see the power God has placed in you. That helps you grow in your faith and confidence with the abilities and gifts He has given specifically to you.

Here are some suggestions to get you started.

- **Learn a new kitchen skill:** Have you ever watched a chef chop a cucumber? It's lightning fast, and those slices are perfectly symmetrical. Picking up a cooking skill like chopping or prepping can boost your kitchen confidence and save you time. And why not make it fun? Picture yourself hosting your own cooking show—apron on, a cute chef's hat, maybe even a new set of knives. "Chop, chop, chop—that's how you dice an onion!"
- **Teach someone a skill you've mastered:** Whether it's gardening, drywalling, playing pickleball, or even folding fitted sheets so they look neat, sharing your know-how helps others gain confidence and also lifts you up.
- **Volunteer your time:** Giving to others boosts confidence because sharing your time, talents, or simply your presence reminds both you and those you serve how deeply valuable and connected we all are.

Conclusion

Go ahead, my friend. Believe in yourself. Believe you are worthy and extremely valuable. Believe you were made with intentionality for a very special purpose. And walk with confidence (in flip-flops or cowboy boots), knowing how much you are dearly loved.

Review and Key Insights to Remember

- Believe is about developing a healthy self-esteem based on your identity in Christ.
- You can walk with assurance knowing that though you may not yet be all God wants you to be, you can Believe you will be.
- You will never feel good enough if you base your self-worth on anything other than your God-given identity.
- Confidence comes when you Believe who God says you are and when you act like you Believe it.
- Developing self-confidence is a skill you can learn by challenging yourself to take small leaps of faith and then repeat the process.

Your Surprise Package Has Arrived!

Meet Beauty and the Green Juice, a vibrant, nutrient-packed drink that hydrates your body, boosts immunity, supports digestion, and nourishes your skin from the inside out. It's beauty in a glass. Just grab your juicer (and maybe a cute pink glass for good measure), and you're all set to glow.

Beauty and the Green Juice

Prep Time: 10–15 minutes
Servings: 1–2

Ingredients:

1 English cucumber, washed and cut into pieces
6 stalks of celery, washed and cut
2 large apples, washed, cut, and deseeded (Honeycrisp if you like it sweeter)
1 lemon, peeled
1 piece of fresh ginger (about 1 inch in size), washed and scrubbed
2 handfuls of fresh spinach

Directions:

Feed all ingredients into the mouth of your juicer. Then pour it over ice in your pretty, pink glass, and enjoy immediately.

Chapter 14

Be Inspired: Time to RSVP

The training was going as I had expected. I was on track running the suggested mileage to prepare for the upcoming marathon. The distances were increasing; I was becoming tired of the long runs and needed every bit of encouragement to help me get through some of those grueling hours hitting the pavement. Because I hadn't run a marathon in over six years, I felt nervous and anxious about it. I knew I needed some extra encouragement, so I sent my mom a text midway through my run, asking her to pray for me. She quickly responded, saying she wished me luck on my run. And with that came the conversation with God that left me completely humbled. But before I go on, I need to back up a bit.

My mom is an 81-year-old German woman who immigrated to Canada when she was 30 years old. She learned English from watching television and never had any formal education to learn the language. She was a stay-at-home mom and avoided all forms of technology—until I gifted her with an old cell phone of mine just a few months before this story. In fact, it's a miracle in itself that she finally tried to learn how to use it. Thank you, Jesus! It has literally changed her life for the better. I could now text my mom and share my progress with her during my run. The experience was such a huge blessing. And to receive a text message from her is still to this day something I never take for granted. That's why when I asked her to pray for me, I was both happy and sad when I received her response.

You see, my mom is not a Christian. When I became a believer as a child, my parents were against my practicing any kind of religion. I grew up keeping my beliefs to myself and eventually not living a life for God. Many years later, as Christ drew me back into a true relationship with Him, my mom began to see some changes in me and over the years came to accept my faith. And that brings us back to my story.

As I received my mom's text, I was happy she was encouraging me and wishing me well. She had never done that for me in this capacity. Yet I was feeling a bit discouraged. My thoughts went from being joyful about her use of technology to being skeptical that she would ever come to know Jesus. And my mind started racing with reasons and excuses for why it might never be possible. She doesn't like to read. English is her second language. She doesn't like to go to church and gets bored and distracted there. If she won't read the Bible or go to church, how will she ever get saved? She won't watch religious shows on TV. She doesn't know how to use the Internet. When I talked to her about Christ, she just changed the subject.

Suddenly, I heard the Holy Spirit intervene. "Bianca, what makes you think I can't soften her heart? Language is no barrier for Me. None of these reasons are even obstacles for Me. I can do anything. All you need to do is keep praying. Don't give up hope. Keep running your race. Leave the rest to Me."

That's when my physical run became fueled by the grace of God, and I realized He was absolutely right. Why was I thinking it was all up to me? If Jesus, through the power of the Holy Spirit, could heal the blind, cure diseases, and rise from the grave after dying on the cross, surely He was able and perfectly capable of doing this as well.

Isn't it ironic how we can outwardly proclaim to believe in miracles and yet within our own personal circumstances doubt that God can make what seems impossible possible? We pray for miracles because we truly want them, but do we pray really believing that they can happen? I have to admit that sometimes it feels like they can happen to everyone except me.

How about you? Do you believe in miracles but doubt if you'll ever really lose the weight? Do you proclaim Jesus can move mountains but doubt your ability to get healthy? Are you inspired by women of great faith in the Bible (Esther, Mary, Deborah, Ruth, Sarah) but discouraged by your lack of faith to trust God in something like weight management? Do you really believe God can help you overcome this battle even though you've struggled with it for years?

The answer to these questions depends heavily on how much you will let the Holy Spirit drive your getting healthy intentions. The truth is that you don't need to pray for a miracle. You already possess the power within you to help propel you forward to the other side of the mountain you're facing. That power comes from the Holy Spirit who lives inside of you if you are a believer in Jesus Christ (Acts 2:38). And do you want to know the best part? The Holy Spirit is waiting for your RSVP so you can see what He can do through you if you really believe it is possible for you, and if you'll take action by applying what you've learned in this book.

Be Inspired is about letting the Holy Spirit guide you toward healthy lifestyle habits and about empowering you to inspire others to do the same. After all, God doesn't just call us to faithfulness; He calls us to fruitfulness. And fruit comes after we've taken action. It's like signing up for a marathon. You don't just register and pay the fee; you actually have to show up for the race and step over the starting line. *That's* when the time chip on your bib gets activated, when you start running forward. All this is to say that faith without action won't give you any results.

"Faith is in your feet, not your feelings."
—Pastor Tony Evans

Restoring the Soul

How can we Be Inspired by the power of the Holy Spirit? First, I think it helps to know exactly who the Holy Spirit is and what He does to help us understand how His power in us can help propel us forward on our journey.

The Bible refers to one God in three persons: God the Father, God the Son, and God the Holy Spirit. All three are God, yet all three are distinct. I think most of us can agree that we know about God the Father and Jesus Christ the Son. We tend to talk about them a lot. But often, the Holy Spirit is someone we kind of put on the back burner. He's there, but we're not always thinking about Him and what He's doing behind the scenes. I'm not saying I can't grasp the concept of who He is. It's just when I'm struggling, doubting, or worrying, I forget about the arsenal of power God has equipped me with, otherwise known as the Holy Spirit.

Many passages throughout the Bible refer to the Holy Spirit and what He does. Since we know that God's Spirit comes to live in our human spirit when we become believers (Rom. 8:16, Acts 2:38), we can be assured that we will never be alone. His Spirit seals us as a child of God and guarantees our eternal life with Him forever (Eph. 1:13-14). God sends His Holy Spirit to assist us with our Christian walk. He is like a companion who forever walks alongside us, guiding us to the truth of God as we journey through life.

The Holy Spirit connects our human spirit to God Himself. This marks how we as believers can have a true personal relationship with the one true God. When the Holy Spirit comes to live within us, He begins the lifelong process of change, making us more Christ-like (2 Cor. 3:18). But He doesn't just help us and guide us; He teaches us (John 14:26), He reminds us of Jesus's words and scripture (John 14:26, John 15:26), He convicts us of sin (John 16:8), He gives us the wisdom to discern (John 16:13, James 1:5), He intercedes for us by praying on our behalf (Rom. 8:26–27), He equips us with every spiritual blessing (Eph. 1:3), and He gifts us with spiritual gifts (1 Cor. 12) to help the body of Christ as we live according to what God has called us to do.

You see, we don't just have the Holy Spirit in us to seal our destiny with God. God has sent His Spirit to empower us to make a difference in this world using His strength and His power. The Holy Spirit gives us the competence and ability that comes supernaturally from the Father so we can handle any task at hand that He has called us to do. And when we utilize the power we already have within us—the Holy Spirit's power—we become unstoppable in living a life that glorifies God.

> *The Holy Spirit gives us the competence and ability to handle any task that He has called us to do.*

That's why when it comes to changing your health and life, if you are not relying on the power of the Holy Spirit, it will be difficult to climb that mountain on your own. The truth is that we need to display His supernatural ability when we walk confidently through our trials and struggles, believing that He has equipped us with everything we need in order to succeed. That is how the glory of God can be displayed, not in our own strength, willpower, and abilities but in accomplishing the impossible through Christ our Lord. He makes the impossible possible. And do you know what *possible* means? It means that it can be done with the power of someone or something.[19] That's right—with the power of the Holy

---

[19] According to the first thing that comes up when you google the meaning of *possible*.

Spirit. "For the Spirit God gave us does not make us timid, but gives us power, love and self-discipline" (2 Tim. 1:7).

How the Fight Is Won

I realize that by now you may be feeling excited about the power of the Holy Spirit. But how do we live out this holy confidence in reality? The key to living it out is to be prepared for the battle well in advance. And for that, we need a little lesson from an underdog turned champ: Rocky. Yes, I'm referring to the character and movie *Rocky*. In my opinion, any of the *Rocky* movies are a great source of inspiration, but let's go all the way back to the first one that came out in 1976.

Here's a brief synopsis, but be warned, there are spoilers if you haven't seen the movie. There's a guy (Rocky Balboa, played by Sylvester Stallone) who dreams of becoming a boxing champ. He's not fancy. He doesn't have a lot of money. And he's an unknown. He hasn't made a name for himself in the world of boxing. But as fate would have it, he's given an opportunity to go head to head with the champion. Some of the most famous scenes in the movie are about Rocky's struggles and hardships through training. You see him pushing through physical limitations to reach a new level of strength, endurance, speed, and power. He's up training at sunrise and still training until sunset. He's exhausted. His body hurts. He wants to quit. But he keeps going. He perseveres. And even while he runs up those famous steps in Philadelphia (a popular scene from the movie) and you see him finally get to the top in victory, you know he would never have gotten up there without three very important things:

1. Help from his trainer who gave him a strategy and accountability.
2. Support and encouragement from his family and friends.
3. Willingness to put faith into action; he had a goal and acted on it by doing the work.

But do you know how the movie ends? Though Rocky trains as hard as he can, he doesn't win the infamous boxing match with Apollo Creed. The point is that this movie isn't great because it's a story about winning. It's great because it's a story of perseverance and hope. It's great because of Rocky's journey of transformation and unstoppable will to get back up even after he's been knocked down. And to quote Rocky in the movie, "But it ain't about how hard you hit. It's about how hard you can get hit and keep moving forward" (Avildsen 1976).

So let me put this into a real-life application. No matter how many times you've tried something and failed, never give up on your dream or goal. To do so would be to give up all hope that God can do what seems impossible. It doesn't matter how many times you've tried a new diet program. It doesn't matter how many gym memberships you've canceled. It doesn't matter that I quit six different taekwondo studios over the course of 17 years until I finally stuck with training long enough to get my first black belt. See? We all have goals and dreams that don't always come easily to us. One of my former taekwondo teachers, said, "The only difference between a white belt and a black belt is that the black belt didn't give up."

Failure does not define who you are. Instead, it should fuel your determination to get up and try again, to keep on persevering, to keep on hoping and dreaming. And remember, you are not in this fight alone. You have the power of the Holy Spirit (your trainer) in you who has equipped you with knowledge (this book) and wisdom (God's Word) to transform you from an underdog to a champion from the inside out. All you need to do is believe it, take action, and keep moving forward.

> *Failure does not define who you are. Instead, it should fuel your determination to get up and try again.*

Beware of Jabs and Punches

As I've mentioned throughout this book, Satan will try anything he can to discourage you from truly forging ahead on this journey. But if you are prepared for his schemes, you can overcome his attacks. It's like studying the way your opponent fights in the ring. If you pay attention, you'll be able to predict what his next moves are going to be, so when they come, you'll know how to block and counterpunch.

You can do this by relying on the power of the Holy Spirit to turn fear into courage (Steps to Change, Chapter 4), knowledge into wisdom (Be Healthy), weakness into strength (Be Active), distraction into focus (Be Mindful), imbalance into steadfastness (Be Kind), blindness into sight (Be Beautiful), doubt into belief (Believe), and self-reliance into God-dependence (Be Inspired). By heeding and applying these principles throughout your journey, you are well prepared to stand against Satan when he comes to knock you down. You have learned these principles and more as we've journeyed together through The B.Losophy Way in this book.

Keep in mind that Satan's attacks aren't always in your face. Sure, he'll try the jab to your chin. But when you block and counterpunch, don't assume he won't be back. He might just sneak up on you with an uppercut. When you find yourself in a struggle or a holding pattern of discouragement, doubt, or discontentment, don't forget the third thing Rocky had in his corner: support from trusted family and friends. Bring them into the ring to fight with you. Because if you think Satan fights fair, know that he doesn't. And you can be sure he has an entourage with him as well. Share your struggle. Ask your team to pray for you. And don't forget to pray for yourself. Then knock Satan out with the power of the Holy Spirit.

Action Step: Save these scriptures so you always have them on hand when you need them.

	Transformation Scriptures	
Fear to Courage (Steps to Change, Chapter 4)	Deuteronomy 31:6	Be strong and courageous. Do not be afraid or terrified because of them, for the Lord your God goes with you; he will never leave you nor forsake you.
Knowledge to Wisdom (Be Healthy)	James 1:5	If any of you lacks wisdom, you should ask God, who gives generously to all without finding fault, and it will be given to you.
Weakness to Strength (Be Active)	Isaiah 41:10	So do not fear, for I am with you; do not be dismayed, for I am your God. I will strengthen you and help you; I will uphold you with my righteous right hand.
Distraction to Focus (Be Mindful)	Proverbs 4:25–27	Let your eyes look straight ahead; fix your gaze directly before you. Give careful thought to the paths for your feet and be steadfast in all your ways. Do not turn to the right or the left; keep your foot from evil.
Imbalance to Steadfastness (Be Kind)	Galatians 5:1	It is for freedom that Christ has set us free. Stand firm, then, and do not let yourselves be burdened again by a yoke of slavery.
Blindness to Sight (Be Beautiful)	1 Peter 3:3–4	Your beauty should not come from outward adornment, such as elaborate hairstyles and the wearing of gold jewelry or fine clothes. Rather, it should be that of your inner self, the unfading beauty of a gentle and quiet spirit, which is of great worth in God's sight.
Doubt to Belief (Believe)	Philippians 1:6 NLT	And I am certain that God, who began the good work within you, will continue his work until it is finally finished on the day when Christ Jesus returns.
Self-Reliance to God-Dependence (Be Inspired)	Jeremiah 17:7	But blessed is the one who trusts in the Lord, whose confidence is in him.

Did I mention that Rocky wins his fights in the rest of the *Rocky* movies (II–V)? Now that, my friend, is how I see your story playing out. Be Inspired by the power of the Holy Spirit living within you, equipping you, gifting you, and calling you to glorify our Heavenly Father through your obedience to live according to the Spirit.

Let's pray.

Dear Heavenly Father,

Lord, I thank You for gifting me with Your Holy Spirit. You know the trials and temptations I face, and You give me the strength to overcome them. When I forget, please remind me of the incredible power and wisdom You've given me through Your Word, and I thank You for those You've placed in my life to support me. You steady my heart and my mind, and You sustain me at all times. Holy Spirit, I worship You for empowering me to live a godly life and walk in full victory over the enemy. Thank You. In Jesus's name, amen.

Restoring the Body

Be Inspired isn't just about living inspired by the Holy Spirit. It's about taking what you've learned in this book, putting it into action, and while doing so, inspiring others to do the same. Be Inspired to be a living example of what it looks like when you put your faith into action.

Use God's power, direction, and discernment in every getting healthy intention you set, whether saying no to unhealthy eating habits or committing to an exercise routine. Whether it's making sleep a priority or taking your stresses to God through prayer, He has equipped you with everything you need. "Praise be to the God and Father of our Lord Jesus Christ, who has blessed us in the heavenly realms with every spiritual blessing in Christ" (Eph. 1:3). That means that in Christ we have all the benefits of knowing God as well as the gifts of the Spirit, and we can enjoy these blessings right now and in eternity.

You might question whether losing weight or getting healthy actually bears fruit for God's Kingdom. Maybe it even seems a bit trivial, like "What does my weight loss have to do with God or His Kingdom?" Well, let me tell you a real-life example of how your actions can have a ripple effect.

A couple months after I wrote the first draft of this book, I was walking along the beach with my husband and my mom. A woman approached me and said I looked fit. She wondered what I was doing to keep in shape, and we started a conversation right then and there. It turned out that the woman was going through a major health crisis, and by what I can only believe was God's way of intervening, I ended up praying for her as my mom and husband stood silently nearby. I don't mention this story to gloat about something I've done. I'm mentioning it because your transformation—yes, even something as trivial as weight loss—could be the very thing that God uses to minister to someone else.

So how do you know your actions won't inspire someone else? When you are struggling and relying on God's strength to persevere, how do you know that the changes in your physical appearance won't prompt someone to ask, "How did you do it?" What would you do? Would you give all the glory to a new diet or exercise program? Or would you give the glory to Jesus? Because in the end, we never know when our testimony will come in handy or who it will benefit.

So, my dear friend in Christ, Be Inspired. Just as the Holy Spirit inspires you to build healthy lifestyle habits, you too can inspire others. That's because He

> *Just as the Holy Spirit inspires you to build healthy lifestyle habits, you too can inspire others.*

who is in you is greater than any chocolate in the world, even the high-end Belgian stuff.

Be Inspired also means sharing what you've learned. Help others find their way back to health, maybe even to Jesus. Live out your faith through the little things like your health journey and the big things like your life journey, and share all of it. Don't wait until you've lost a few pounds to feel confident. Start believing you are worthy now, and you'll start acting like it. Share your journey with others as you walk through it, just like Rocky did. Because the truth is, it's the struggle and the journey of perseverance and hope that's inspiring, not just the successful outcome.

Here's what I used to say at the end of class in my boot camp: "Be the inspiration you want to be." I know that never made sense, but it was meant to say, "Be the inspiration you want to have in your life." Somehow, my boot campers always knew what I meant. Thanks, ladies!

But I think this sounds better: "Be the inspiration He (God) wants you to be."

And if you could say a little prayer for my mom, that she may come to know Christ in a deep and meaningful way, I'd really appreciate it.

Take Action Now: Be the Inspiration He Wants You to Be

- Share this book with family and friends or gift them a copy of their own. Yes, even men can benefit from it.
- Invite family and friends to join you on your health journey.
- Be a mentor to others regarding healthy living while you are transforming.
- Create an in-person or online group to be accountable to one another along this journey.

- Create a group at church who can read this book and journey together.
- Keep rereading this book as often as you like, but especially when discouragement, doubt, or discontentment comes knocking on your door.
- Sign up for more support, encouragement, and upcoming programs on my website at BiancaSchaefer.com and follow me on social media for daily inspiration.

If this book has inspired you, please leave a helpful review on Amazon to help share its blessing with others.

Final Words

Throughout the journey of reading this book, you've learned the various strategies, tools, and B.Losophy principles designed to integrate your spiritual, mental, and physical health. You know exactly what to do and how to reach your healthy living destination. All you need to do now is keep taking it one step at a time. With your focus on your spiritual health at the forefront, allow the Wellness Whisperer to guide and fuel you—from the inside out—to bring you across a new threshold of what it means to have a healthy body, mind, and spirit. I can't wait to see you on the other side, holding your arms up like a champ.

Bianca, xoxo

Now to him who is able to do immeasurably more than all we ask or imagine, according to his power that is at work within us, to him be the glory in the church and in Christ Jesus throughout all generations, for ever and ever! Amen.

—Eph. 3:20–21

Review and Key Insights to Remember

- Be Inspired is about letting the Holy Spirit guide you toward healthy lifestyle habits and about empowering you to live in a way that inspires others to do the same.
- The Holy Spirit gives you the competence and ability to handle any tasks He has called you to do. Rely on His power to help you throughout this journey.
- Be prepared for setbacks, but don't let them define you. Instead, it should fuel your determination to get up and try again.
- Let the Holy Spirit remind you of what you have learned—how to turn fear into courage (Steps to Change, Chapter 4), knowledge into wisdom (Be Healthy), weakness into strength (Be Active), distraction into focus (Be Mindful), imbalance into steadfastness (Be Kind), blindness into sight (Be Beautiful), doubt into belief (Believe), and self-reliance into God-dependence (Be Inspired).
- Share your B.Losophy journey. Take action now, get support, and be the support for others.

Your Surprise Package Has Arrived!

I couldn't possibly let you journey through this book without a little dessert at the end. I hope you'll agree it was worth the wait. I hope you'll enjoy it as much as I do.

Blissful Blueberry Nice Cream
I'm definitely not against dairy, but sometimes my tummy prefers a break. This nice cream is a delicious dairy-free treat that's packed with antioxidants, fiber, and healthy fats, making it a satisfying dessert that's gentle on your digestion. And trust me, it's so tasty that even dairy lovers will want a second scoop.

Prep Time: 5 minutes
Servings: 2

Ingredients:
2 cups frozen blueberries
1½ cups coconut milk, extra if needed
1 ripe avocado, peeled, pit removed
1 tsp. vanilla extract
Optional: 1 tsp. freshly squeezed lemon juice
A few fresh blueberries for garnish

Directions:
Place all ingredients in a high-powered blender and mix until smooth. This has a very thick consistency, so add a bit more coconut milk if needed. Serve in a bowl and top with fresh blueberries for garnish. Enjoy!

30 Easy-to-Implement Nutrition Tips

1. Prep veggies when they're fresh. Store cut-up veggies in see-through glass containers and place them at eye level in your refrigerator.
2. Portion fish, meat, and poultry so you can cook only what you need, especially if you live alone or have a small family. Don't freeze the whole Costco value pack or you'll be eating chicken for breakfast, lunch, and dinner when you thaw it out.
3. Instead of butter, margarine, or mayonnaise, use hummus or avocado.
4. Eat more veggies, and always include them in your smoothies.
5. If you want to reduce dairy intake but not go cold turkey, use coconut, almond, cashew, oat, or hemp milks in your smoothies instead of yogurt.
6. Nutritional yeast or ground cashews make wonderful parmesan cheese substitutes.
7. If you eat meat, poultry, and fish, choose hormone-free, raised without antibiotics, wild, and sustainably sourced.
8. Eat less meat by choosing to eat plant-based meals more often. Try Meatless Monday once a week.

9. Create a menu for the week and go grocery shopping with a list. Review your menu the night before and prep whatever you can in advance if you're busy in the week ahead.
10. Swap refined sugar with maple syrup, raw honey (in small amounts), or alternative natural sweeteners such as monk fruit or stevia.
11. Swap vegetable oil with coconut or olive oil.
12. Clean your fridge and freezer at least twice a year. Toss out old condiments that just take up space in your fridge. Also, toss out brown bananas you haven't used or any expired, freezer-burned items.
13. Do a pantry raid at least once a year. Do you really need all those cans, pastas, baking items, and spices you rarely use? Toss expired items and don't restock your pantry with stuff you don't need.
14. When making a new recipe, prep all your food, herbs, spices, cooking utensils, and dishes before you start cooking so they're ready to go when you start. Use a book or tablet stand.
15. Get a good set of knives and keep them sharp.
16. Be prepared for a hunger emergency. I regularly keep raw nuts or a mini Kind bar in my purse. I seldom need to eat them, but having them there for emergencies has helped when I've needed a little something to keep me going.
17. Take healthy snacks with you if you're traveling or heading out to run errands for the day. I don't know how many times I've said I would grab a bite on the go and then was unable to find a healthy, affordable option. If hunger suddenly strikes, you'll have something on hand to tide you over until you can choose what's best for you. And if you find something you would rather eat instead, just take your food home and eat it later.

30 EASY-TO-IMPLEMENT NUTRITION TIPS

18. Make extra food for leftovers or neighbors in need.
19. Set the table. Use napkins. Put on some relaxing dinner music. Use small plates. Say grace. Eat slowly. Breathe. Enjoy your meal with company or in peaceful solitude.
20. Swap dark chocolate for milk chocolate at least sometimes.
21. Ditch the microwave popcorn and make popcorn on the stove; use coconut oil.
22. Eat fruit when you crave something sweet.
23. Set a timer on your phone reminding you to drink water throughout the day.
24. At the end of the day, ask yourself, "Did I eat any vegetables today?"
25. Add nuts, seeds, and fiber to smoothies and salads regularly.
26. Not sure what to do with the rice and beans in your cupboard? Make bowls. Use the rice as the base, add tablespoons of beans, lentils, or chickpeas, top with lettuce or whatever veggies you have on hand, sprinkle on some nuts and seeds, and add a salad dressing. Eat the extra cooked rice and beans for breakfast in a burrito the following day.
27. Add more herbal tea to your daily or weekly routine. Substitute an afternoon coffee with green tea or hot water with freshly squeezed lemon and ginger.
28. If you buy food you absolutely don't like, don't force yourself to eat it. Give or donate it to someone else.
29. Keep your kitchen counters clean and free of clutter. Find a place for your mail, purse, keys, and so on.
30. Replace sugary drinks with infused water alternatives. Add fresh-cut strawberry slices and mint to filtered water, let it sit (or cool) for an hour or two, and enjoy.

Special Thanks

To my Lord and Savior Jesus Christ. No amount of thank yous will ever be enough for all You've done for me. You've rescued, restored, and sustained me in ways only You could. Every good thing in my life is because of You. You are my strength, my joy, my anchor, and my peace. I love You. All glory belongs to You.

To Phil, my one true love. You've journeyed with me through 10 years of writing this book. From idea to inception, from defeat to triumph you've been there, cheering me on from the very beginning. I know you've always believed in me, even when you may have wondered if I'd ever actually finish. You are a man of patience, and I love you for it. Thank you for giving me the space to grow and the time I needed to believe in myself as much as you believed in me.

To Andrea and Nicole, thank you for welcoming me into your family. I'm deeply blessed to have you both as stepdaughters. Your kindness, love, and support mean more than words can say. I love you both dearly.

Lauren, is "thank you" even enough? Through all the years and tears, your encouragement has carried me through my lowest lows. Thank you for every four-hour conversation and every text, voice memo, card, prayer, and unwavering belief in me. Only God could have orchestrated a coffee craving that brought us together beyond the lineup. I love you, sweet, sweet friend. Matt and Ila too.

To my prayer warriors Amy, Brandi, and Janet. Knowing I have friends and sisters in Christ who faithfully go before the Lord on my behalf is life-changing. Thank you for your perseverance in prayer and for your loving friendship. You've listened, comforted, encouraged, and stood with me. I'm so grateful for the unique ways God brought each of you into my life. XOXO.

Marie, my wonderful sister-in-law, thank you for offering me the peace and quiet of your beautiful cottage to write. Your support has meant so much, and I love you dearly.

To Mama, Sigrid, Thomas, Harry, Shelley, Bock, Mom and Dad Bedell, Sherri, Rob, Chantel, Paul, Corry and so many more friends I couldn't possibly name. You gave me the gift of time. Writing requires long stretches of quiet and focus, and you allowed me the space to disappear for weeks and months to pour my heart into this project. Thank you for your love, patience, and understanding.

To Pastors Terry Hoskins and Casey Nowlin at Family Church in Marco Island, Florida, and Pastor Ed Clements at Church on the Queensway in Toronto. Thank you for your guidance, encouragement, and prayers.

To Jane and Reverend Larry Schmidt. Thank you for your prayers and unwavering support. We met on Marco Island the year I began writing my very first draft of this book. I remember saying, "I'm here to write a book," and your encouragement since that day has meant so much. Thank you for believing in me and covering me in prayer. Your friendship has been a true blessing.

To Cathie Ostapchuk and Vanessa Hoyes. Your leadership and wisdom have been truly inspiring. The way you lead with boldness and authenticity, with humility and grace has impacted me more than I could ever put into words. Thank you for the encouragement you've poured into my life.

To Wendy Chiavalon, my editor at *The Local Biz Magazine*, thank you for reaching out all those years ago and inviting me to write. You've made me a better writer, and I'm so grateful for you.

And to the team at Lucid Publishing, thank you for your encouragement, wisdom, and patience throughout this process. I truly couldn't have asked for a better team.

References

"Air Masses: Safety Spotlight: Air Masses and Fronts." AOPA. Accessed March 17, 2024. https://www.aopa.org/training-and-safety/online-learning/safety-spotlights/weather-wise-air-masses-and-fronts/air-masses.

Aleman, Ricardo Santos, Marvin Moncada, and Kayanush J. Aryana. "Leaky Gut and the Ingredients That Help Treat It: A Review." *Molecules* 28, no. 2 (2023): 619. https://doi.org/10.3390/molecules28020619.

Allberry, Sam. *What God Has to Say About Our Bodies: How the Gospel Is Good News for Our Physical Selves*. Wheaton, IL: Crossway, 2021.

"The Average Woman Spends 17 Years of Her Life on Diets." Medical Daily. September 18, 2012. https://www.medicaldaily.com/average-woman-spends-17-years-her-life-diets-242601.

Avildsen, John G., dir. *Rocky*. Chartoff-Winkler Productions. 1976.

"Beauty & Personal Care – Worldwide." Statista. Accessed March 17, 2024. https://www.statista.com/outlook/cmo/beauty-personal-care/worldwide.

Burack, Emily. "Read America Ferrera's Powerful Monologue in *Barbie*." *Town & Country* online. August 5, 2023. https://www.townandcountrymag.com/leisure/arts-and-culture/a44725030/america-ferrera-barbie-full-monologue-transcript/.

Charlies-Names.com, entry for *Bianca*, accessed 2024, *Charlies-Names.com* (2024), "Bianca is an Italian name of Germanic origin. What does the name Bianca mean? Bianca means 'white' and 'fair' (from Germanic 'blanc')"

Chu, Brianna, Komal Marwaha, Terrance Sanvictores, Ayoola O. Awosika, and Derek Ayers. "Physiology, Stress Reaction." *StatPearls*. May 7, 2024. https://www.ncbi.nlm.nih.gov/books/NBK541120/.

Clear, James. *Atomic Habits: An Easy & Proven Way to Build Good Habits & Break Bad Ones*. New York: Avery, 2018.

Cooper, Geoffrey M. *The Cell: A Molecular Approach*. 2nd Edition. Sunderland, MA: Sinauer Associates. https://www.ncbi.nlm.nih.gov/books/NBK9838/.

Du, Hongfei, Ronnel B. King, and Peilian Chi. "Self-Esteem and Subjective Well-Being Revisited: The Roles of Personal, Relational, and Collective Self-Esteem." *PloS One* 12, no. 8 (2017): e0183958. https://doi.org/10.1371/journal.pone.0183958.

"Eye Candy Definition." Your Dictionary. Accessed March 17, 2024. https://www.yourdictionary.com/eye-candy.

Gooley, Joshua, J., Kyle Chamberlain, Kurt A. Smith, Sat Bir S. Khalsa, Shantha. M. W. Rajaratnam, Eliza Van Reen, Jamie. M. Zeitzer, Charles, A. Czeisler, and Stephen W. Lockley. "Exposure to Room Light Before Bedtime Suppresses Melatonin Onset and Shortens Melatonin Duration in Humans." *The Journal of Clinical Endocrinology and Metabolism* 96, no. 3 (2011): E463–72. https://pubmed.ncbi.nlm.nih.gov/21193540/.

"How Laughter Can Relieve Stress + Ideas to Laugh It Off." University of St. Augustine for Health Sciences. Accessed March 17, 2024. https://www.usa.edu/blog/how-laughter-can-relieve-stress/.

"The Jerusalem Archaeological Park–Davidson Center." iTravelJerusalem. Accessed March 17, 2024. https://www.itraveljerusalem.com/attraction/davidson-center-jerusalem#overview.

REFERENCES

Kendrick, Alex, dir. *Overcomer*. 2019. Affirm Films, Provident Films, Kendrick Bothers. DVD.

Kendrick, Stephen, and Alex Kendrick. *Defined: Who God Says You Are*. Nashville: B&H Publishing, 2019.

Kim, Tae Won, Jong-Hyun Jeong, and Seung-Chul Hong. "The Impact of Sleep and Circadian Disturbance on Hormones and Metabolism." *International Journal of Endocrinology* 15 (2015). https://doi.org/10.1155/2015/591729.

Koziarz, Nicki. *5 Habits of a Woman Who Doesn't Quit*. Nashville: B&H Publishing Group, 2016.

Leaf, Dr. Caroline. *Cleaning Up Your Mental Mess: 5 Simple, Scientifically Proven Steps to Reduce Anxiety, Stress, and Toxic Thinking*. Grand Rapids: Baker Books, 2021.

Levinson, Cheri A., Rowan A. Hunt, Caroline Christian, Brenna M. Williams, Ani C. Keshishian, Irina A. Vanzhula, and Christina Ralph-Nearman. "Longitudinal Group and Individual Networks of Eating Disorder Symptoms in Individuals Diagnosed with an Eating Disorder." *Journal of Psychopathology and Clinical Science* 131, no. 1 (2022): 58–72. https://doi.org/10.1037/abn0000727.

Maxwell, John C. "The Secret of Your Success Is Determined by Your Daily Agenda." Instagram. December 14, 2023. https://www.instagram.com/reel/C02vlk9OLFL/.

"The Meaning of Kind in English." *Cambridge Dictionary* online. Accessed March 17, 2024. https://dictionary.cambridge.org/us/dictionary/english/kind.

"Methods for Voluntary Weight Loss and Control: NIH Technology Assessment Conference Panel." *Annals of Internal Medicine* 116, no. 11 (1992): 942–9. https://doi.org/10.7326/0003-4819-116-11-942.

Neumark-Sztainer, Dianne, Melanie Wall, Nicole I. Larson, Marla E. Eisenberg, and Katie Loth. "Dieting and Disordered Eating Behaviors from Adolescence to Young Adulthood: Findings from a 10-Year Longitudinal Study." *Journal of the Academy of Nutrition and Dietetics* 111, no. 7 (2011): 1004–11. https://doi.org/10.1016/j.jada.2011.04.012.

"Orthorexia." WebMD. September 16, 2024. https://www.webmd.com/mental-health/eating-disorders/what-is-orthorexia.

Rahman, Saidur, Khandkar Shaharina Hossain, Sharnali Das, Sushmita Kundu, Elikanah Olusayo Adegoke, Ataur Rahman, Abdul Hannan, Jamal Uddin, and Myung-Geol Pang. 2021. "Role of Insulin in Health and Disease: An Update." *International Journal of Molecular Sciences* 22, no. 12 (2021): 19. https://doi.org/10.3390/ijms22126403.

Runfola, Cristin D., Ann Von Holle, Sara E. Trace, Kimberly A. Brownley, Sara M. Hofmeier, Danielle A. Gagne, and Cynthia M. Bulik. "Body Dissatisfaction in Women Across the Lifespan: Results of the UNC-*SELF* and Gender and Body Image (GABI) Studies." *European Eating Disorders Review* 21, no. 1 (2013): 52–9. https://doi.org/10.1002/erv.2201.

Schaefer, Bianca. 2019. "The Scoop on Poop: Your Health Depends on It." *The Local Biz Magazine.* Spring 2019. https://www.thelocalbizmagazine.ca/archives/LB201901-WEB.pdf.

"Schaefer Family History." Ancestry.com. Accessed March 19, 2024. https://www.ancestry.com/name-origin?surname=schaefer.

"Self Esteem." BetterHealth Channel. Accessed March 19, 2024. https://www.betterhealth.vic.gov.au/health/healthyliving/self-esteem.

Selye, Hans. "Stress and the General Adaptation Syndrome." *British Medical Journal* 1, no. 4667 (1950): 1383–92. https://doi.org/10.1136/bmj.1.4667.1383.

REFERENCES

Stanley, Charles F. *When the Enemy Strikes: The Keys to Winning Your Spiritual Battles.* Nashville, TN: Thomas Nelson, 2004.

Thau, Lauren, Jayashree Gandhi, and Sandeep Sharma. "Physiology, Cortisol." StatPearls. August 28, 2023. https://www.ncbi.nlm.nih.gov/books/NBK538239/.

"Three Out of Four American Women Have Disordered Eating, Survey Suggests." *Science Daily.* April 23, 2008. https://www.sciencedaily.com/releases/2008/04/080422202514.htm.

Upenieks, Laura. "Unpacking the Relationship Between Prayer and Anxiety: A Consideration of Prayer Types and Expectations in the United States." *Journal of Religion & Health* 62 (2022): 1810–31. https://doi.org/10.1007/s10943-022-01708-0.

Van Braam, Hailey. 2024. "White Color Psychology and Meaning." Color Psychology. February 22, 2025. https://www.colorpsychology.org/white/.

van Egmond, Lieve T., Elisa M. S. Meth, Joachim Engström, Maria Ilemosoglou, Jasmin Annica Keller, Heike Vogel, and Christian Benedict. "Effects of Acute Sleep Loss on Leptin, Ghrelin, and Adiponectin in Adults with Healthy Weight and Obesity: A Laboratory Study." *Obesity* 31 no. 3 (2022): 635–41. https://doi.org/10.1002/oby.23616.

Vig, Himanshu, and Roshan Deshmukh. "Weight Loss and Weight Management Diet Market Size, Share, Competitive Landscape and Trend Analysis Report, by Product Type (Better-for-You, Meal Replacement, Weight Loss Supplement, Green Tea, and Low-Calorie Sweeteners) and Sales Channel (Hypermarket/Supermarket, Specialty Stores, Pharmacies, Online Channels, and Others): Global Opportunity Analysis and Industry Forecast, 2021–2027." Allied Market Research. 2021. https://www.alliedmarketresearch.com/weight-loss-management-diet-market.

"What Are El Niño and La Niña?" National Ocean Service. 2023. https://oceanservice.noaa.gov/facts/ninonina.html.

"What She Said." Adelle Davis Foundation. Accessed March 19, 2024. https://www.adelledavis.org/adelle-davis/what-she-said/.

"Why Stress Causes People to Overeat." Harvard Health Publishing. February 15, 2021. https://www.health.harvard.edu/staying-healthy/why-stress-causes-people-to-overeat.

Wondmkun, Yohannes Tsegyie. "Obesity, Insulin Resistance, and Type 2 Diabetes: Associations and Therapeutic Implications." *Diabetes, Metabolic Syndrome and Obesity* 13 (2020): 3611–16. https://pubmed.ncbi.nlm.nih.gov/33116712/.

"Writing About Emotions May Ease Stress and Trauma." Harvard Health Publishing. October 11, 2011. https://www.health.harvard.edu/healthbeat/writing-about-emotions-may-ease-stress-and-trauma.

"Your Digestive System and How It Works." National Institute of Diabetes and Digestive and Kidney Diseases. 2017. https://www.niddk.nih.gov/health-information/digestive-diseases/digestive-system-how-it-works.

Zorn, Justin, and Leigh Marz. "Neuroscience: The Busier You Are, the More You Need Quiet Time." *Harvard Business Review*. March 17, 2017. https://hbr.org/2017/03/the-busier-you-are-the-more-you-need-quiet-time.

www.ingramcontent.com/pod-product-compliance
Lightning Source LLC
Chambersburg PA
CBHW070648170426
43200CB00010B/2156